# Hockey Drills
## for
# Puck Control

**Vern Stenlund, EdD**
University of Windsor
Huron Hockey School

**Human Kinetics**

Library of Congress Cataloging-in-Publication Data

Stenlund, K. Vern
    Hockey drills for puck control / K. Vern Stenlund.
      p.    cm.
    ISBN 0-87322-998-3
    1. Hockey--Training.   2. Hockey--Offense.   I. Title.
    GV848.3.S74   1996
    796.962'07--dc20                         96-14562
                                                 CIP

ISBN: 0-87322-998-3

Copyright © 1996 by K. Vern Stenlund

**Developmental Editor:** Kirby Mittelmeier; **Assistant Editors:** Chad A. Johnson, Kent Reel, and Sandra Merz Bott; **Editorial Assistant:** Amy Carnes; **Copyeditor:** Bonnie Pettifor; **Proofreader:** Bob Replinger; **Text Designer:** Judy Henderson; **Layout Artist:** Tara Welsch; **Photo Editor:** Boyd La Foon; **Cover Designer:** Jack Davis; **Photographer:** Gerry Marentette; **Illustrator:** Dianna Porter; **Mac Art:** Accurate Art, Inc.; **Printer:** Versa Press

Human Kinetics books are available at special discounts for bulk purchase. Special editions or book excerpts can also be created to specification. For details, contact the Special Sales Manager at Human Kinetics.

Printed in the United States of America    10  9  8  7  6  5

**Human Kinetics**
Web site: www.HumanKinetics.com

*United States:* Human Kinetics, P.O. Box 5076, Champaign, IL 61825-5076
800-747-4457
e-mail: humank@hkusa.com

*Canada:* Human Kinetics, 475 Devonshire Road, Unit 100, Windsor, ON N8Y 2L5
800-465-7301 (in Canada only)
e-mail: orders@hkcanada.com

*Europe:* Human Kinetics, 107 Bradford Road, Stanningley
Leeds LS28  6AT, United Kingdom
+44 (0) 113 255 5665
e-mail: hk@hkeurope.com

*Australia:* Human Kinetics, 57A Price Avenue, Lower Mitcham, South Australia 5062
08  8277 1555
e-mail: liahka@senet.com.au

*New Zealand:* Human Kinetics, P.O. Box 105-231, Auckland Central
09-523-3462
e-mail: hkp@ihug.co.nz

To all my coaching mentors, colleagues, and teaching associates who have inspired and provoked. Thank you for taking the time to share both your knowledge of and love for this great game.

# Contents

# Foreword

Good skating, stickhandling, passing, scoring, and defense don't happen by accident. Hockey players and teams do these things well because they *work* at them. Even the greatest athletes in the world—many of whom I've coached in professional hockey—become great *players* only if they are willing to practice countless hours to develop and refine their skills.

Drills, if executed correctly and efficiently, are among the best practice activities a player can perform. The number of repetitions and the variety of game-like challenges a player can get with a drill far surpass the learning opportunities of any other practice activity. As they say, perfect practice makes for perfect performance.

While flawless performance may be unrealistic to expect, it should always be a goal. Junior players are not likely to approach that goal, but by practicing drills like the ones in *Hockey Drills for Puck Control*, even young players can develop rapidly.

Author Vern Stenlund has seen from both a player's and coach's perspective what good drills and a good work ethic can do. He was an overachieving player whose professional career was cut short by injury. Since then, he has coached and instructed players at all levels—and he is clearly one of the finest teachers in hockey today.

In this book, Vern takes you very systematically through the progression of first-rate puck-control skills. If puck control sounds too basic or boring to you, remember that too many players never develop this skill fully and then pay the price when they're on the ice.

These drills require work, but don't forget to have some fun while you're doing them. Most of the drills have a competitive component: You can try to beat your previous best performance or score, your opponent, or both. And if you don't come out on top, keep after it until you do, because *that* is the first step in the development of any hockey star.

Tom Webster
Assistant Coach, Philadelphia Flyers

# Acknowledgments

This book would never have been possible without the assistance of the following people: Marie Hawkins, who brought the original draft to print; Ted Miller and Kirby Mittelmeier, for their guidance and humor; All the support people at Human Kinetics—a world-class organization; Brent Webster, John IIoy, and Wayne Jacklin, my colleagues in Leamington, thank you for your input and ideas; Harold Konrad because "he's the man"; Paul O'Dacre at Huron Hockey—"they broke the mold" (thank goodness!).

And finally, to my wife and children for putting up with my "author, author" routines! Your love and support is cherished.

# Key to Diagrams

| | |
|---|---|
| X or O | Player/opposing player/pair of players |
| C/L | Coach or leader |
| D | Defenseman |
| F | Forward |
| G | Goaltender |
| → | Forward skating |
| ∿∿→ | Skating with puck |
| ----► | Passing |
| = or ‖ | Stopping |
| ⟹ | Shooting |
| ◦◦◦◦◦ | Backward skating |
| ‖‖‖‖‖‖‖‖ | Lateral skating |
| ℓ | Turns |
| ℓ | Tight turns |
| ⌒ | Pivots (forward to backward/backward to forward) |
| ⋮ | Pucks |
| △ △ | Pylons (cones) |

# Introduction

The game of hockey has evolved at all levels in recent years, moving steadily away from a sport of brute strength to one of greater skill and precision. Today's hockey coaches seek players reaching for their potential, players with highly developed skills who can contribute to a team's development and success. Those seeking to advance into hockey's more competitive leagues must continually improve their skills.

One such invaluable skill involves controlling the puck in a variety of situations. By improving puck control skills, players will not only increase their enjoyment of the game but also improve their opportunities for advancement. This book is designed to provide you, the player or coach, with practical suggestions for mastering puck control.

By mastering the drills and concepts presented in these pages, players will learn to use puck control as a powerful tool in determining the outcome of a game. Often you will hear successful hockey coaches say, "If you keep control of the puck, they can't score on you." Mastering puck control puts players in a position to control the flow of a game by controlling who has possession of the puck the longest. This way teams can become more successful—even when their opponents are bigger or stronger.

Practicing the drills in this book will also help players improve their game performance. Why? Because the activities are designed to help develop practical skills that relate directly to game situations. You will immediately begin to see the benefits of the drills in competitive games—just as coaches at the Huron Hockey School have over the years of developing this method of teaching.

Players and coaches alike can use the drills in this book to guide individual and group practice sessions. What's more, the activities are useful for all levels of coaching and beneficial to all players—from the youngest beginner to the most experienced all-star at the highest level of the sport. This is, however, more than just another "drill" book. I've also included valuable tips and ideas for each activity that will help players and coaches dramatically reduce the time required to master a skill.

In assembling the drills for this book, I have given special attention to providing simple activities that beginners will find "do-able" almost immediately, allowing players at any level to achieve a measure of success. Then, I give guidelines for ways to "refine" the drills in order to provide more experienced players a greater challenge. This is often accomplished by changing time and space parameters of the drills, an intensifying technique that forces players to improve their skills and progress. As players' skills increase, so too will their ability to perform the activities at a faster pace using less space. They will know their puck control skills have improved because they will be able to see and feel the results.

As you look at the individual drills in this book, pay special attention to the "Key Points" section of each activity. In this section are many helpful ideas and suggestions to assist you in perfecting the drills. Years of teaching and coaching experience have gone into developing these activities, and the comments that accompany them reflect the approaches of the many coaches who have come through the Huron hockey program, some of whom have reached the professional level. Their advice will serve you well as you continue along the road to mastering puck control.

# Roller Hockey

Roller hockey enthusiasts will find many of the drills in this book easily adaptable to a nonice environment. It's important to realize, however, that certain skills reinforced through ice hockey drilling patterns may be affected by factors such as increased friction and different playing materials. If you intend to incorporate some of the drills into your roller hockey practice, simply try the drill and modify it as necessary. Any problems you might encounter will quickly become evident and adjustments can then be made.

# How the Book Is Organized

The drills have been assembled with some specific objectives in mind. The first one is basic but especially important: Rather than combining drills from all phases of the game of hockey, this book looks at one major aspect of play, namely, moving toward a high level of puck control. This was done in order to avoid one of the pitfalls that many coaches and players encounter when they either purchase a book or video filled with new drills or attend a hockey seminar or clinic, and, armed with a wealth of new information, come home ready to conquer the world. What they inevitably realize is that many instructional materials are overly complicated and do not provide players appropriate drills for their specific skill levels. Often the result is confusion and frustration for everyone involved.

In keeping with the purpose of providing a useful and meaningful resource, this book does not attempt to provide drills for all situations— the game of hockey is far too complex. What it does offer are varied and flexible drills that incorporate other aspects of the game, such as passing or turning, as a part of puck control activities. When designing an effective practice session, coaches and players should emphasize the specific objectives for each particular drill.

Second, this book presents a level of progression from simple activities at the beginning of each chapter to more difficult drills at the end of each chapter. On a larger scale, the same philosophy applies, with each succeeding chapter of the book offering more challenging activities. In providing this progression, a wider range of players and coaches will find material presented here practical and useful, regardless of skill level.

Third, some chapters have specific sequences of drills that build upon one another. Working through these sequences will allow players to understand more clearly the objectives of the drills and to master the skills faster. I've also included sample practice plans so coaches and players can see how the drills can be integrated into practice sessions. To make practice planning easier, go to the Drill Finder section at the end of the book to identify other aspects of play incorporated by specific drills.

As you look through the book, you will notice that I've included a chapter on passing. In this section, many of the drills use the skill of passing as a foundation of puck control. Although the inclusion of passing might appear inconsistent with the traditionally held view of what constitutes puck control, many veteran coaches would argue that players often attempt to do too much individually when they have possession of the puck, resulting in unwanted turnovers. That is why I've reinforced the key concept of "give and go"—not as a single component of passing and receiving, but more important as an integral part of any team's puck control strategy. By learning this concept, players will realize that puck control means more than simply holding onto a puck for as long as possible. In turn, many problems historically associated with players who "hog" the puck can be controlled, helping to eliminate many a coach's worst nightmare.

Little reference is made throughout book to shooting. Of course, the end goal in hockey is to score goals and rarely is this objective accomplished without shooting. However, since the main focus of this book is puck control, aspects of how the drills relate to shooting have not been discussed or diagrammed in great detail. For those coaches and players wishing to integrate shooting and puck control drills, I've suggested ways to modify individual drills to include a shot at the end of the activity. Shooting, as well as other specific hockey skills, are to be the focus of later books in this series.

Finally, you will notice that the drills rarely require extra equipment or substantial amounts of set-up time. Most require only a stick, a puck, and some ice. As a result, they can be done with a minimum of wasted time and effort so you can spend valuable ice time doing the activities, not discussing them.

# 1 Principles of Puck Control

In this chapter we will examine some basic principles essential to the improvement of your puck control skills. These principles represent the foundation of your puck control development, and everything that follows in this book is based upon the assumption that you have read and understand these principles. As you progress through the different drill patterns, check yourself against these basic rules of puck control, and your ability to advance will be greatly enhanced. As with all other skill areas, practice is essential if success is to follow.

## Principle #1: Find the Right Stick for <u>You</u>

An important, yet often overlooked, part of developing superior puck control skills lies in the hockey stick you use. With the new technologies available to stick manufacturers today, your options have increased dramatically as to the type, size, and shape of sticks to choose from. Where once only wooden sticks were available to players, now they can choose from a variety of makes and models composed of high-tech materials such as graphite, kevlar, and aluminum. When choosing a stick, players should consider their needs and style of play.

With all the options to choose from, it's important to try as many different sticks as possible to find the right match. You may find you prefer aluminum sticks to traditional wood or a more flexible shaft to a less flexible shaft. For example, someone who primarily uses a wrist shot will want to find a stick with more flex in the shaft than a player who prefers slap shots. A cheap way of experimenting with different stick types is to borrow teammates' sticks at practice. No absolute rules for selecting your hockey stick exist, but before you choose one, you should consider the following factors.

## Stick Lie

It is important to have as much of the stick blade as possible on the ice to develop sound puck control skills, and stick lie will affect this greatly. The lie of a stick refers to the angle formed by the shaft and the blade. The higher the lie number for a stick, the more upright the stick—and you—will be when the blade is flat on the ice.

Lie numbers generally range from four to seven, although custom-made sticks may go as high as eight or nine. If you tend to skate slightly hunched over at the waist in the style of Wayne Gretzky, you will require a lower lie number, such as four or five. Players who skate more upright should seek a stick with a higher lie number.

A good way to check whether you're using a stick with the correct lie is to examine the bottom of the blade often to ensure that it is wearing evenly, not just on the heel or toe portion.

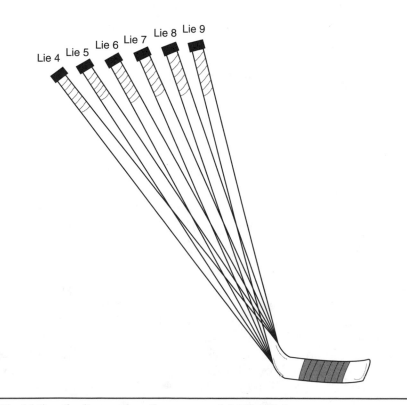

The higher the lie number, the more upright the stick.

Stick lie greatly affects a player's skating stance—the higher the lie number, the less bending at the waist.

## Stick Length

Stick length has a dramatic effect on puck control by determining puck position relative to your body: A longer shaft forces the puck farther away. The position of the puck can be an important factor for puck control, depending on your strengths as a player, so it's important to try different lengths for comfort and puck control. The length of your stick will also directly impact your shooting technique. The old adage that your stick should be cut at the same level as your nose or chin is not valid. Instead, experiment with different stick lengths to find the right fit for your game.

## Blade Curvature

A common mistake made by younger players is to use a stick with more curvature than they are ready for—something that can actually hinder development of puck control skills. Many choices of blades exist. For beginners, however, I generally recommend a blade with less curvature. Only once you have established sound puck control habits should you attempt to work with a blade that has greater curvature. A good rule for coaches to follow is "the younger the player, the straighter the blade."

Consider stick lie, stick length, and blade curvature before choosing the hockey stick that is right for you. You should take as much care when choosing a hockey stick as a baseball player takes when choosing a bat.

# Principle #2: Learn Proper Hand and Arm Positioning

To effectively control a puck, players must understand the importance of proper hand, arm, and stick position relative to the body. First, hands should be a comfortable distance apart on the shaft of the stick. The farther down the shaft you place the lower hand, the more bent at the waist you become. Most important, the arms must be away from the

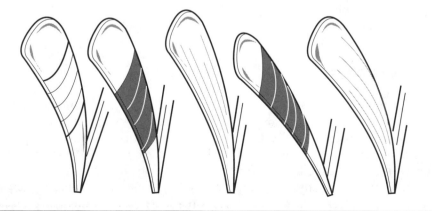

It's important to choose a blade shape that fits your skill level: Less experienced players should use a straighter blade.

body to control the puck. This is especially true in game situations. If a player has "lazy arms," keeping them too close to the body, the puck will inevitably find its way into the skates where control becomes difficult.

Player with possession in top drawing shows improper hand and arm positioning, with stick and puck close to the body and head down. This is a dangerous position to be in as a defender approaches. Proper positioning is shown in the bottom drawing: hands away from the body, arms extended, head up, ready to attack.

# Principle #3: Head and Shoulder Movements Affect Puck Control

In game situations, hockey players must be ready to change direction rapidly. Many players do not appreciate how much the head and shoulders affect the speed and puck control with which they turn. The most efficient way to begin a turn is by simply turning your head. That way your shoulders, arms, and stick automatically follow. So, rather than attempting to start a turn by moving the puck in another direction with the stick, it is more useful to get into the habit of first "looking up ice." Many of the drills in this book encourage players to apply this simple principle.

For most efficient turning, get into the habit of first looking up ice—shoulders, stick, and puck will automatically follow.

# Principle #4: Develop a "Feel" for the Puck by Moving Beyond Your "Comfort Zone"

Accomplished pianists do not have to concentrate on (or even look at) the keys on a piano to perform. With a great deal of practice, their finger movements become "second nature." Likewise, hockey players must develop a "feel" for the puck—an automatic connection between the puck on the ice and their fingers on the stick. Then they can concentrate on the skill, drill, or activity they are attempting. The ability to stand still and control a puck with your eyes closed is a good indicator that you have begun to establish a "feel" for the puck.

Once players refine this concept of "feel," they are on the road to puck control mastery and can begin to turn their attention to more game-related matters. Test yourself and challenge your puck control skills. Push yourself past your comfort zone where you are in total control and move to a point where puck control is not a conscious effort but a simple reflex action.

# 2 Fundamental Drills

All of us have heard the old saying "You must learn how to walk before you can run." This concept is reflected in the progressive approach to teaching found in this book. In this chapter, we provide basic puck control drills that can be used for either introducing or reviewing puck control skills. The drills can be used for assessing skills as well. For example, a coach might use these activities early in the season to determine the relative skill level of his players. Players might use the drills to test how accurately and quickly they are able to control a puck in a noncontact environment. As with all the activities in this book, the key is to find the use that best fits your specific goals and needs.

As you use these drills, keep in mind the principles of puck control detailed in chapter 1 to ensure proper progress. If you find any of these drills too difficult, try simplifying them so you can achieve a measure of success. As your skill level increases and the drills become easier, move on to more challenging ones. It makes no sense to consistently include drills in practice that are either too simple or too demanding. Either extreme can result in frustration.

The drills in this chapter, like those found in the rest of the book, can be used at almost any level and are presented progressively from simple to difficult. I have included guidelines for making each drill more challenging for advanced players. Remember that while it might be tempting to skip ahead to some of the more difficult drills initially, it is important for developing well-rounded puck control skills to master the basic drills first. Even professional players spend time practicing the basics in their day-to-day workouts!

# 1 STAND PAT

## Purpose

- To introduce or review basic principles of proper puck control technique
- To assess puck control skill level

## Equipment   None

## Time   2-3 minutes, depending on skill level

## Procedure

1. Players gather at one end of the ice (or, if the group is exceptionally large, on half of the ice, center red line to goal line).
2. Leader (coach or player) demonstrates puck handling activities, moving the puck from front to side while continuously stickhandling the puck.
3. Players must imitate what the leader demonstrates.

## Key Points

- Players should shift weight from left leg to right leg and back again as the puck moves from side to side (e.g., when puck is on left side of body, weight should be on the left side as well).
- Practice principles of puck control, especially hand and arm location.

## Drill Progressions

- Add more difficult activities (e.g., on one knee, on both knees, on stomach) while handling the puck.
- Players should look at the ceiling or close their eyes while handling the puck in order to develop "feel" for puck movement and positioning.

# STAND PAT 1

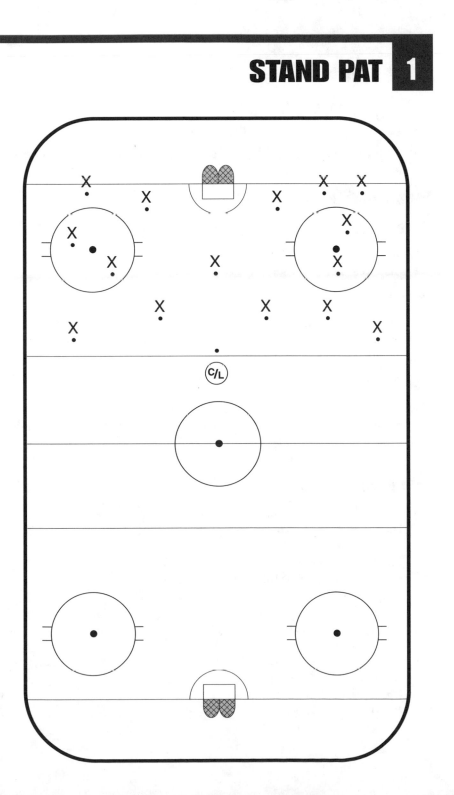

# 2  THE EGG

## Purpose

- To introduce basic puck control skills and identify players' skill levels

## Equipment   Pylons (optional)

## Time   2-4 minutes

- 30-second sets, five sets maximum
- Brief rest between sets (approximately 20 seconds)

## Procedure

1. Players place gloves (or pylons or pucks) shoulder-width apart in front of them on the ice, then must work the puck in a "figure eight" motion through the gloves.

## Key Points

- Players should have (a) proper hand location on stick, (b) arms away from hips, (c) entire blade of the stick on ice, (d) knees bent, and (e) feet stationary.
- Coaches can circulate to assist players where needed.

## Drill Progressions

- Move gloves apart to approximately five feet; this forces players to shift their weight.
- Have players count the number of times they can go through the "egg" in 30 seconds, then reduce time to 25 seconds while trying to maintain the same number of repetitions.
- Have players close their eyes or look at the ceiling while attempting the drill.

# THE EGG 2

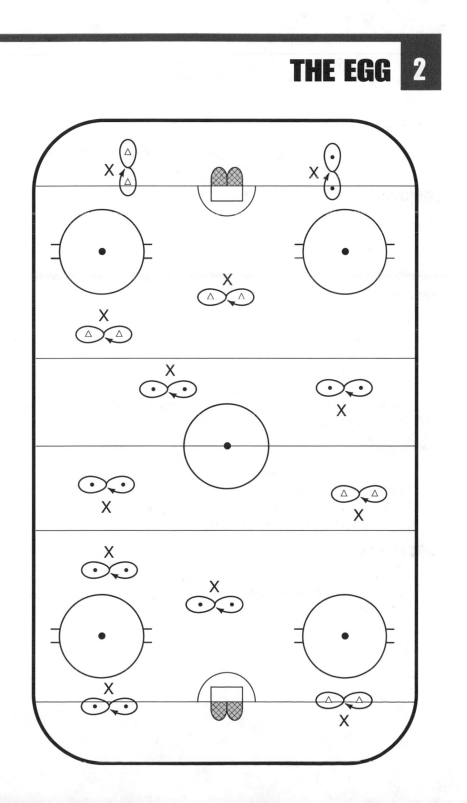

# 3 SKATING THE EGG

## Purpose

- To introduce movement to puck handling skills and include all basic elements of puck control in a noncontact drill

## Equipment   Pylons (optional)

## Time   2-4 minutes

- 10- to 15-second sets; three to five sets
- Rest period not to exceed 30 seconds between sets

## Procedure

1. Players skate through the egg (see drill #2), pivot, and go backward while handling the puck, attempting to keep control of the puck at all times.
2. For the first part of the drill, players skate *forward* through middle of the egg, *backward* around the outside.
3. For the second part of the drill, players skate *backward* through middle, *forward* around the outside.

## Key Points

- Keep head up; try glancing down only to locate the puck.
- Watch for "lazy arms" (hands and arms too close to the body). Keeping hands and arms away from the body will help keep the puck from ending up in the skates.

## Drill Progressions

- Increase skating speed through the drill or shorten time frame.
- Have another player pass the puck to players coming up the middle of the egg.

# SKATING THE EGG 3

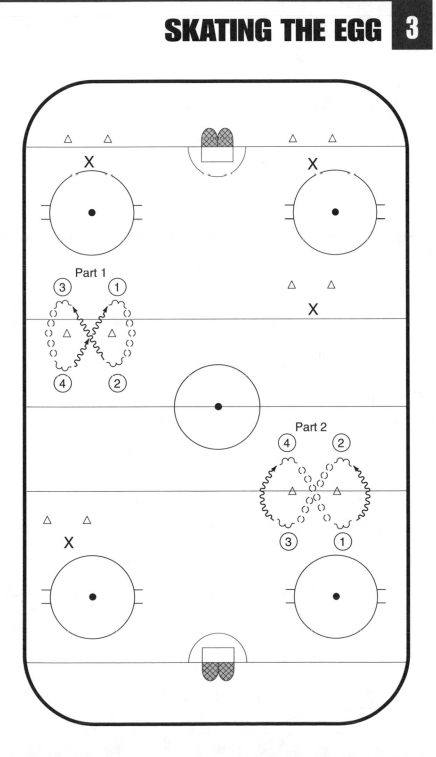

# 4  FOLLOW THE LEADER

## Purpose

- To force players to focus their attention forward (or "up ice") rather than down at the puck
- To provide a way for many players to actively work on basic puck control skills all at once

## Equipment   None

## Time   3-5 minutes, depending on group size and skill level

## Procedure

1. Group should be set in "waves" (lines) numbering from one to six (or more with bigger group) at the end of the ice.
2. As each wave of players moves forward, coach (or player) indicates where they are to skate with the puck (sideways, backward, or stop and handle the puck), changing on the whistle.
3. Leader uses his hand or stick for commands and can develop his own system of gestures for specific instructions.

## Key Points

- Vary the routine to practice the basic principles and make the drill challenging.
- Start with simple activities, then increase difficulty with each new wave.

## Drill Progressions

- Use half-ice format (if more than one leader is available), increasing the number of repetitions per player.
- Increase the rate of whistle changes, forcing players to react more quickly.
- Have players choose a partner and "mirror" activities on their own.

# FOLLOW THE LEADER  4

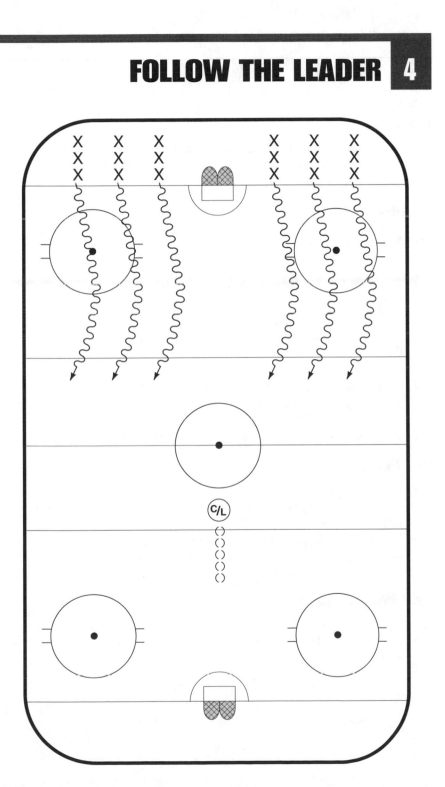

# 5 | THE IMITATOR

## Purpose

- To reinforce basic puck control skills development
- To encourage creativity and enjoyment while working on basic puck control skills

## Equipment   None

## Time   2-4 minutes

- 30-second sets; up to five maximum
- 10-second rest between sets as leaders change

## Procedure

1. Players should be in groups anywhere on the ice.
2. One player is leader and all others must "imitate" what the leader does.
3. Leader demonstrates unique activities for the others to attempt, such as skating backward, sideways, pivoting, and turning. Encourage leaders to be creative.
4. When the whistle blows, a new player takes over as leader.

## Key Points

- Transition between leaders should be done quickly, to emphasize that puck handling is tiring when done to excess (a warning for potential "puck hogs").
- Leaders should push others past their skill "comfort zone" by trying things that are not "normal" (e.g., using only one hand on stick, one skate on ice, on back, knees, and so on).

## Drill Progressions

- Move from slow- to fast-paced activities or shorten time frame.
- Do one activity only; then next leader must build upon the last activity.

# THE IMITATOR 5

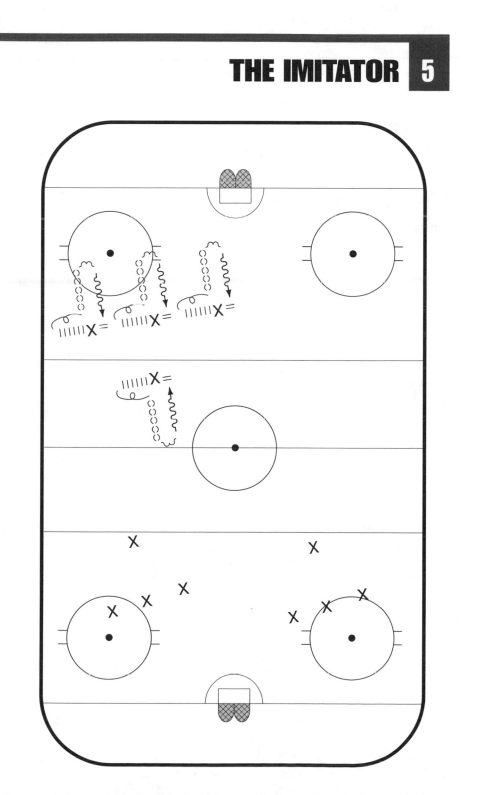

# 6 CIRCLE DRILLS

## Purpose

- To provide the opportunity for players to work in a confined area on puck control basics

## Equipment   None

## Time   4-5 minutes

- 15- to 30-second sets; five to seven sets maximum
- Rest 10 to 15 seconds beween sets

## Procedure

1. Players take positions around face-off and center ice circles.
2. On the whistle, all groups skate the circles, performing a specific activity as directed by the coach.

## Key Points

- Begin with very simple actions such as handling the puck while skating forward; change direction on whistle.
- As the drill progresses, actions become more difficult (e.g., drop to one knee on whistle, then up; drop to two knees on whistle, then up).

## Drill Progressions

- Use only one puck for the group, so passing becomes a part of the drill.
- Add a second puck to make this a "wake-up" drill.
- Advanced players should add pivots, backward skating, and other more difficult actions.

# CIRCLE DRILLS  6

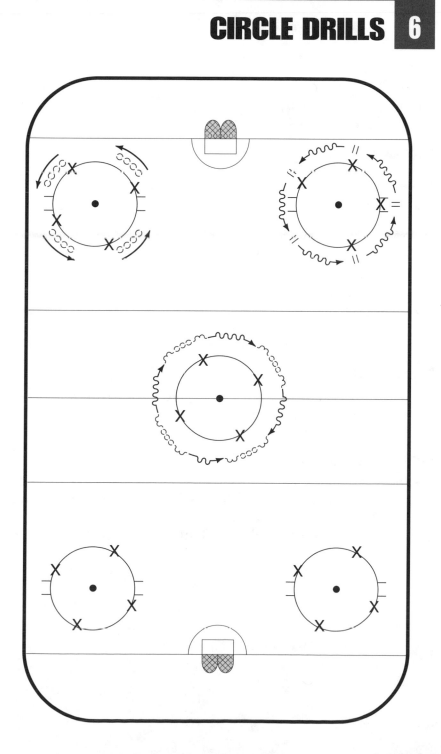

## 7 FACE THE FLAG

### Purpose

- To reinforce puck handling skills on all sides while skating either forward or backward

### Equipment   None

### Time   3-5 minutes, depending on skill levels

- Four to six repetitions total
- Rest 10-15 seconds between reps

### Procedure

1. Players must skate around the five face-off circles while always facing only one end of the ice.
2. Players should pivot from forward to backward and vice versa while controlling puck.
3. Players go one after another in a single line.

### Key Points

- Players should have enough room between them to ensure recovery time if a mistake is made.
- Demonstrate the route to follow to help players understand.

### Drill Progressions

- Decrease time frame.
- Have players work in pairs, with second partner doing the same pivots but chasing the first player.
- Player with puck must skate and protect puck from partner.

# FACE THE FLAG 7

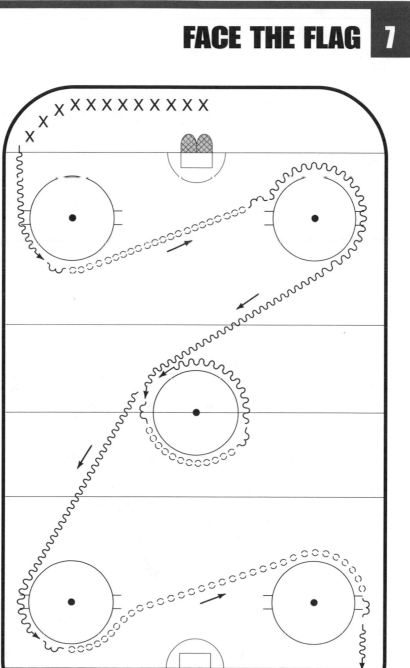

# 8 DOME DRILL

## Purpose

- To force players into puck control situations that call on basic skills

## Equipment   None

## Time   3-5 minutes

- Six repetitions maximum
- Keep drill high tempo, beginning next rep as soon as previous one is concluded

## Procedure

1. Player skates from corner to just beyond the nearest blueline and must pivot with the puck.
2. Drill begins at both ends at once on the whistle.

## Key Points

- Ensure players lead into the pivot or turn by turning their heads.
- Drill starts from one corner then from the other. Players are forced to improve puck handling on "weak side" as well as strong.

## Drill Progressions

- Demand higher speed and more pivots throughout the route skated.
- Have players drop to one or both knees, then recover as quickly as possible.
- Add obstacles for players to work through and around.
- For more advanced levels, have players from both ends exchange pucks during the drill by passing across the ice. This will take practice and patience from both players and coaches.

# DOME DRILL 8

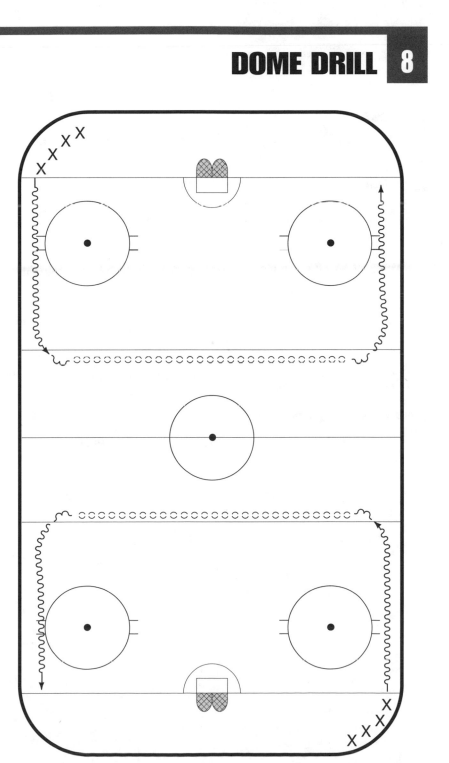

# 9 THE SNAKE

## Purpose

- To reinforce proper edge control during skating, creating the need to handle the puck while feet are continuously in motion

## Equipment   None

## Time   3-5 minutes, depending on skill level

## Procedure

1. Players form a single line and skate around the ice, using a three-stride crossover motion (three strides one way, three strides in the other direction) giving the effect of a snake in motion.
2. Sets should be done while skating both forward and backward.

## Key Points

- Players must keep both feet and hands moving at the same time.
- Don't glide in the corners; keep the legs moving at all times.

## Drill Progressions

- Have players work in pairs, with trailing partner harassing puck carrier in front by hitting the gloves and arms.
- Skate backward.

# THE SNAKE 9

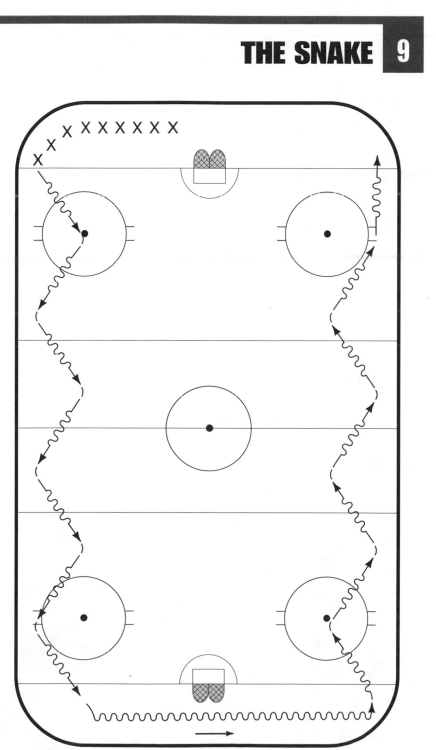

# 10 PUCK CONTROL PIVOTS

## Purpose

- To provide turning practice using proper head and shoulder rotation

## Equipment   None

## Time   3-5 minutes

- Three to five sets; keep players moving

## Procedure

1. Players come out three at a time, each with a puck.
2. At side board, all must pivot and go in other direction toward the other side of rink.
3. Once first group pivots, next group begins, with two pivots each per set.

## Key Points

- Players are forced to pivot in both directions.
- Remember the importance of "looking up ice" in order to turn more quickly.

## Drill Progressions

- Increase the number of repetitions to create a conditioning factor.
- One player acts as a back-checker in group to try to strip the puck from the other two players.
- Use one puck only, adding a passing dimension.

**Going into the pivot**   ➤   **Coming out of the pivot**

# PUCK CONTROL PIVOTS 10

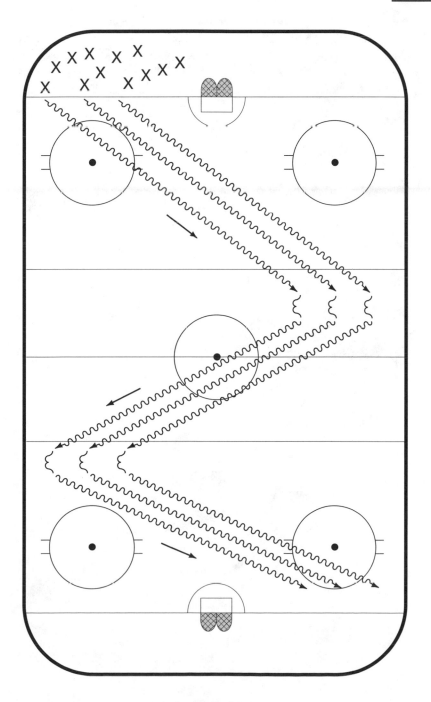

# 3 WARM-UP ACTIVITIES

People associated with athletics generally agree that warm-up activities are important to decrease the number of needless injuries that occur during practices or games. A warm-up and stretching routine enhances flexibility and prepares the body for the quick movements and great stresses that occur in hockey.

For our purposes, the warm-up phase of any practice should serve two specific goals. First, players can use this time to increase their body core temperatures so they are ready for the more demanding workout to follow. This physiological warm-up, which can take up to twenty minutes of your practice time, is important and shouldn't be neglected. Second, coaches or players can choose activities and drills that specifically address the overall objectives of the practice session. This is commonly called a sport- or skill-specific warm-up and provides the basis for the drills reviewed in this chapter. For example, perhaps a coach wants to develop a practice around improving individual skills with puck control as a central theme, or a player wishes to try a difficult skill without having to execute it at game speed.

You can use the following drills as warm-up activities or you can easily alter their difficulty to suit your particular needs. Remember, however, that warm-up is a time to begin building momentum and intensity for the rest of practice and that drills used during this time should reflect this intended progression. Don't expect players to go through high-intensity drills the moment they step on the ice—even if they have stretched before practice.

## 11 STRETCH N' GO

### Purpose

- To provide players an opportunity to stretch while working on puck control skills

### Equipment   None

### Time   3-5 minutes

**Neck and shoulder stretch**

### Procedure

1. Leaders start at each blue line.
2. Players first skate along one side of the ice (side *A* in diagram) and imitate various stretches that leader *A* demonstrates while they continue to handle the puck.
3. On side *B*, players perform specific puck handling exercises as demonstrated by leader *B*.

### Key Points

- Be creative in attempting different actions and vary activities from practice to practice.
- Always loosen muscle groups from the head to the waist, then follow with lower body stretches.

**Wrist stretch**

### Drill Progressions

- Have players attempt the same routines skating backward.
- Have players close their eyes for the puck handling portion.
- Have players work in pairs and add passing as a part of the activity.

**Groin stretch**

# STRETCH N' GO 11

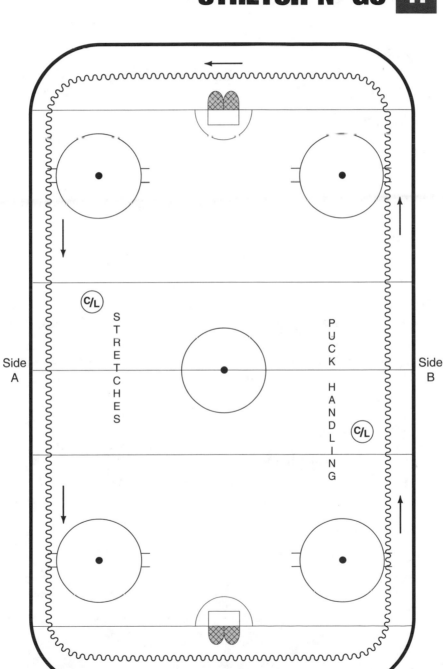

Side A

Side B

C/L

STRETCHES

PUCK HANDLING

C/L

# 12  PIVOT WARM-UP

## Purpose

- To provide a simple workout activity that includes both puck handling and pivoting skills while skating

## Equipment   Eight to 10 pylons

## Time   2-3 minutes

## Procedure

1. Each player has a puck and skates forward through the pylon course, making sure to keep hands and feet in motion.
2. At the bottom of the far face-off circle, players pivot and skate backward down the wall until reaching the far end.
3. One pivot forward, and the player is ready to go again.

## Key Points

- Players should not push or drag the puck, but rather handle it during the entire drill.
- Players should keep their heads up, especially during the backward portion of the activity.

## Drill Progressions

- Increase speed component of the drill.
- Have players pass to partners in another line during the pylon (forward) portion of the drill.
- Turn the activity into a shooting drill at either end.

# PIVOT WARM-UP 12

#  13 ALLEY-OOP!

## Purpose

- To force players to continue moving their feet while handling the puck in turning situations

**Equipment**  Eight pylons

**Time**  3-4 minutes

## Procedure

1. Players begin in four lines at one end of the ice.
2. They must control the puck while making a loop turn around two pylons, making sure to change the direction of the turn at each pylon.
3. Stagger the start to allow room in the turn (once the first player in line makes the first loop, the next player can then begin).

## Key Points

- It is not a race, but a challenge to see if players can gain rather than lose speed around a corner.
- Players should remember to rotate their heads and shoulders earlier for quicker turns.

## Drill Progressions

- Add backward pivots on each turn so players face one end at all times (see drill #7).
- Add a shot on goal to finish the drill.
- Have players do the entire drill while skating backward.

# ALLEY-OOP! 13

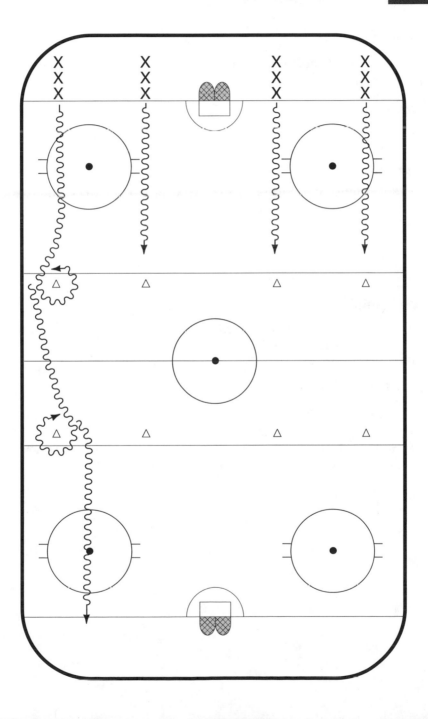

# 14 SKATE THE LINES

## Purpose

- To allow players to experiment with different moves during a puck control warm-up drill

## Equipment    Three pylons

## Time    3-4 minutes

## Procedure

1. Set pylons in middle of ice to split surface into halves lengthwise.
2. A player from each line moves forward on the whistle with puck and must skate the pattern shown.
3. Players should be creative in the way they skate and handle the puck across the lines (for example, shifting the puck from side to side or from front to back while skating).

## Key Points

- Start with easy moves and then follow with more difficult activities according to the skill level of players.
- Watch for the basics: head up, puck in front.

## Drill Progressions

- Start the drill from knees, back, stomach, and so on and make it a race between the two groups.
- Second player must act as back-checker who follows the puck carrier and tries to strip the puck away.

# SKATE THE LINES  14

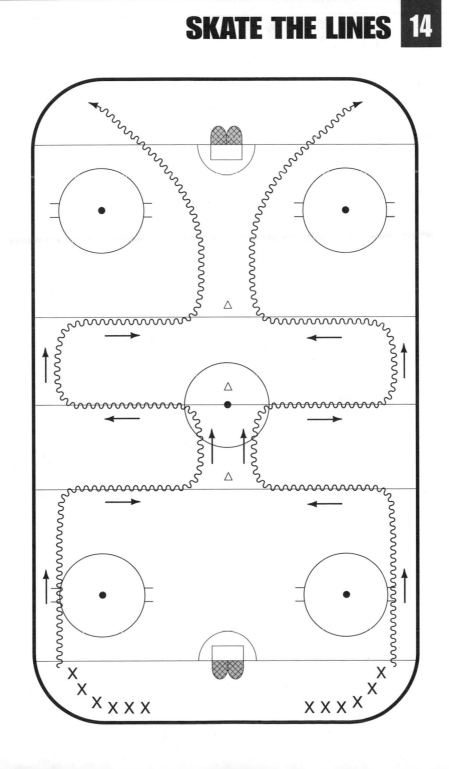

# 15 DOT TURNS

## Purpose

- To reinforce puck control skills in tight turn situations

## Equipment   None

## Time   3-4 minutes

## Procedure

1. Players begin by making 180° turns around dots and pylons as shown in side *A* (a total of six turns) while handling puck (players can use glide or crossover turns).
2. Once all players have gone, the second set involves 360° turns around the dots (see side *B*).

## Key Points

- Players must turn to both their strong and weak sides in this drill.
- Shoulders should not dip; instead, the knees should bend in the turns.

## Drill Progressions

- Add a player as chaser to drill to increase speed.
- Set up two lines on each side and add four pylons. As drill progresses this time, players go in pairs and try to complete eight to ten passes before drill is finished.
- Have players pivot backward at bottom of circle, always facing the same end of the rink.

# DOT TURNS 15

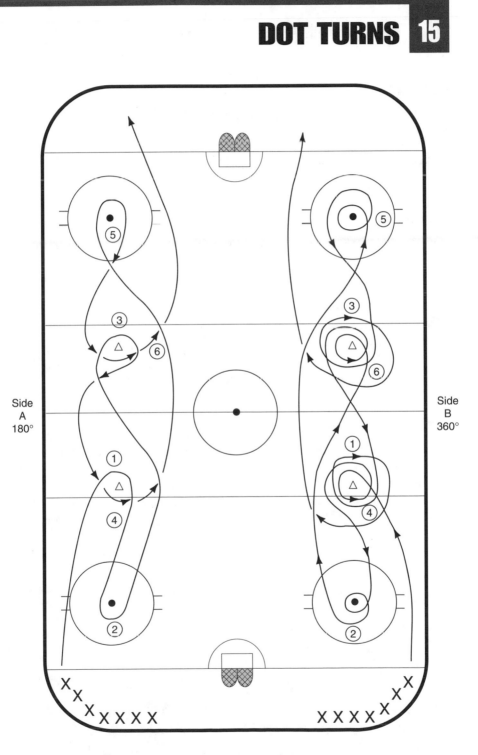

Side
A
180°

Side
B
360°

# 16 QUICK FEET AND HANDS

## Purpose

- To provide practice changing direction quickly while handling the puck

## Equipment   None

## Time   1-2 minutes

## Procedure

1. Players skate leisurely around the rink.
2. On whistle, players take three quick steps forward, STOP, take three quick steps backward, STOP, pivot and go three more quick steps forward; then relax until next whistle.

## Key Points

- This drill is short in duration, so players should work hard at accelerating, stopping, and handling the puck.
- This will improve and promote quickness while controlling the puck.

## Drill Progressions

- Have players attempt a variety of actions including dropping to their knees on the whistle, using the puck in their skates once during sequence, and so on.
- Add a partner so players can work on timing.
- Remember to alter direction during the activity.

# QUICK FEET AND HANDS 16

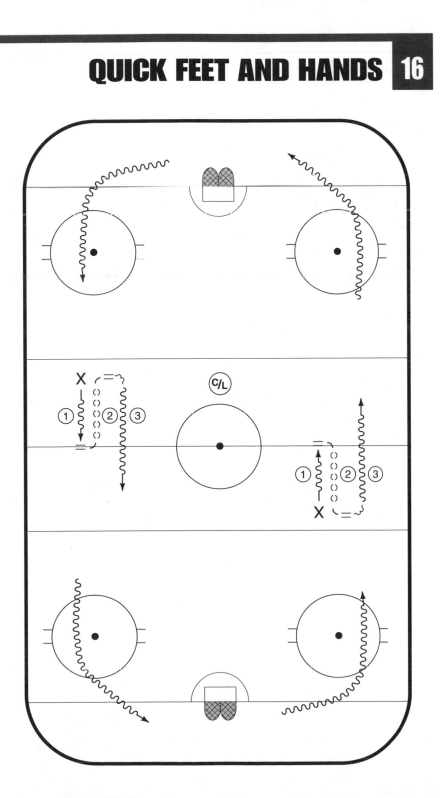

# 17 FOUR BLUES

## Purpose

- To practice puck control and skating while "thinking" through a drill

## Equipment   None

## Time   4-5 minutes

## Procedure

1. Players are in one of four groups situated at the blue lines along the boards. Opposite sides go on the whistle and must follow the patterns demonstrated by the leader while handling the puck.
2. Use pivots, backward, and forward skating.

## Key Points

- Three or four variations of this drill can be attempted to force players not only to demonstrate puck control skills but also to listen and think.

## Drill Progressions

- Add a shot at end of drill.
- Change from having opposite lines going together to same side going on the whistle.
- Have opposite groups pass to players as they come out of pivots.

# FOUR BLUES 17

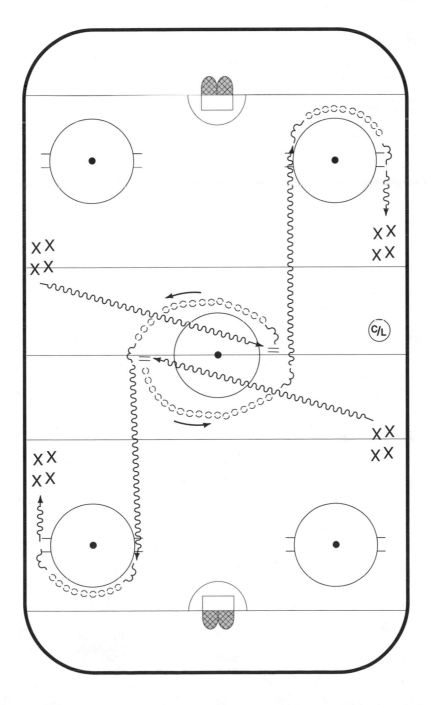

# 18  CANADIAN SKILL WARM-UP

## Purpose

- To promote enjoyment during warm-up while players test their puck control proficiency

## Equipment   None

## Time   3-4 minutes

## Procedure

1. Begin by having leader in center ice doing activities that players attempt to imitate as they skate around the ice.
2. Do stretching and puck handling, increasing difficulty as time goes on.
3. Speed and direction may be altered and feet should be used for controlling the puck as well.
4. Use boards to combine passing and puck control by having players pick up loose pucks in their skates and transfer to their stick.

## Key Points

- Have players try "toeing" the puck with the stick or kicking the puck from skate to stick.
- For safety reasons, players are not allowed in the middle of the ice—this is the leaders' area.

## Drill Progressions

- Add pylons and designate a route to follow.
- All drills should be attempted while skating backward as well.
- Add a partner to increase difficulty with one puck between the pair.

"Toeing" the puck

# CANADIAN SKILL WARM-UP 18

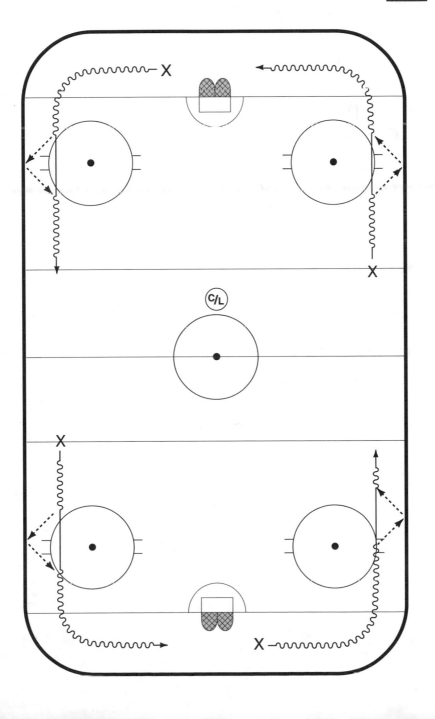

# 19 NOAH'S WARM-UP

## Purpose

- To work on puck control skills while skating forward and backward

## Equipment  None

## Time  2-3 minutes

## Procedure

1. Leader designates what pattern should be followed on each half of the ice (one forward, one backward).
2. Players line up in pairs at blue line one and follow in close order, creating a nonstop warm-up activity.

## Key Points

- Players switch lines when they cross blue line two.
- Emphasize foot movement in conjunction with puck control work (there should be little gliding in this drill).

## Drill Progressions

- Increase the intensity and speed of the activity.
- Add pivots during different times. Leader can blow whistle; all players must pivot and go.

# NOAH'S WARM-UP 19

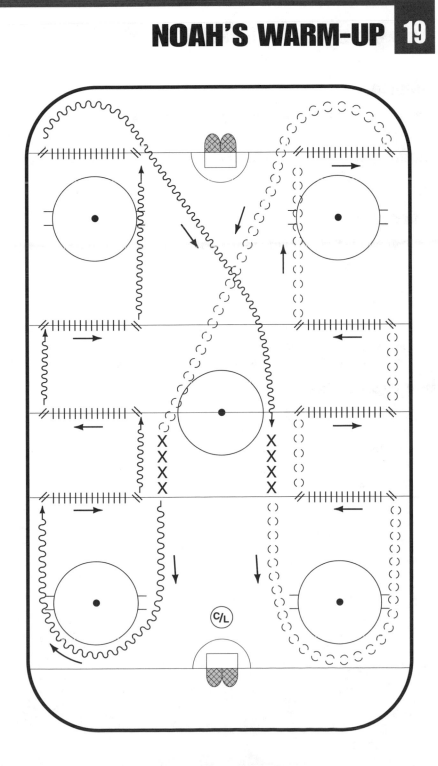

# 20 OBSTACLE COURSE WORKOUT

## Purpose

- To provide a fun exercise to get players loose and ready for practice

**Equipment**   Eight pylons, or sticks, chairs, trash cans, or the like

**Time**   4-5 minutes

## Procedure

1. Set up obstacles around the ice as shown.
2. Players go through the circuit as directed by the leader. This is not a race; the emphasis should be on technique and precision.

## Key Points

- Use whatever materials are available to set up different obstacles: a hockey stick over two pylons, a trash can from the arena, or a group of chairs. Players will welcome anything different.

## Drill Progressions

- Add more obstacles at shorter distances to set up tighter turns.
- Have players compete with individual time trials to increase intensity.

# OBSTACLE COURSE WORKOUT 20

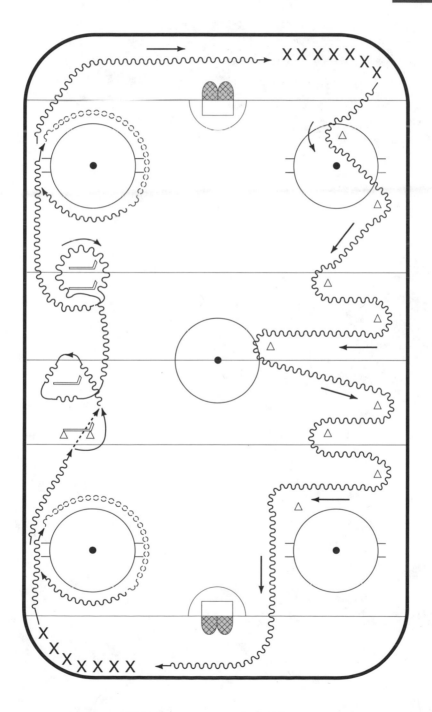

# 4 Passing Drills

As hockey has evolved over the past several decades, the concept of puck control has taken on a different meaning. In today's highly developed game, it is rare indeed to find a player who will consistently go end-to-end with a puck. Instead, puck control now includes a broader range of skills that go beyond the stickhandling ability of an individual. Today's interpretation of puck control includes passing and receiving the puck as a means of achieving a team puck control advantage.

Many teams use passing as a way of maintaining puck control—whether on the attack, in transition, or while playing in their own defensive zone. Knowing when to give up possession of the puck to a teammate to keep team possession is a skill that can be taught and reinforced through drills. For some players, the thought of giving up the puck to maintain puck control might be a foreign one. How many times have we heard coaches complain about players who consistently "hog" the puck? If players can master the concept of "give-and-go" early in their development, these kind of problems can be avoided.

While we will not examine the techniques of passing and receiving in great detail in this chapter, several of the activities incorporate passing to help players and teams maintain puck control over their opponents.

# 21 SNAKE SHADOW

## Purpose

- To practice passing and timing to maintain puck control

## Equipment   None

## Time   2-3 minutes

## Procedure

1. Players skate around the rink in pairs cutting hard to one side with three strides, then back in the other direction for three strides, passing as they go.
2. Players should stay close to each other, no more than 10 feet apart, concentrating on timing and accuracy of passes.
3. Sets can be done both forward and backward.

## Key Points

- This activity was seen previously (see drill #9) and is easily adapted for passing.
- Timing is a problem players must work on from the first step.
- Players may use boards as a means of puck possession.

## Drill Progressions

- Add a chaser.
- Use boards in passing sequence. Dump off the boards instead of going directly to the stick blade with the pass.

# SNAKE SHADOW 21

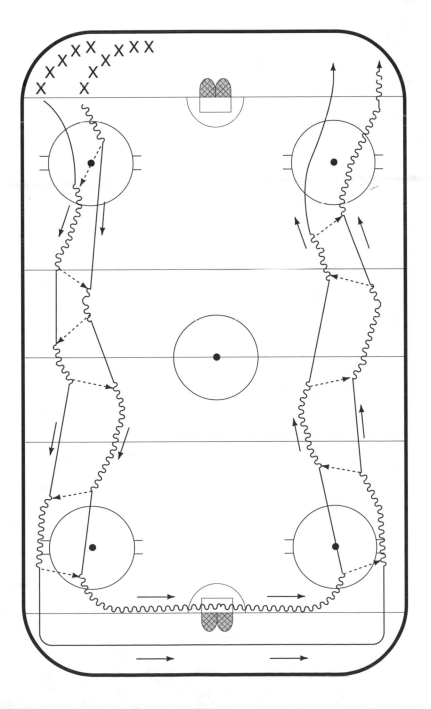

## 22 TURN AND GO

### Purpose

- To teach the concept of "give-and-go" in passing as a means of puck control
- To practice puck control skills while skating into and out of a turn

### Equipment   None

### Time   2-3 minutes

- Two or three sets only

### Procedure

1. Players begin in four lines at one end of the rink.
2. Player from line A skates with puck and makes a tight turn between the center red line and closest blue line.
3. Player passes back to first person in line B, then receives pass while heading up ice.
4. Line B begins next, using line C for their passing partners.

### Key Points

- Last group (line D) passes back to line C, and the drill comes back the other way (C to B, B to A).
- Players should call for the puck as they exit the turn.

### Drill Progressions

- Add pivots (180° or 360°) as players head up ice.
- Include two or three full turns (one in each zone).
- No gliding during turns; keep both feet moving at all times.

# TURN AND GO 22

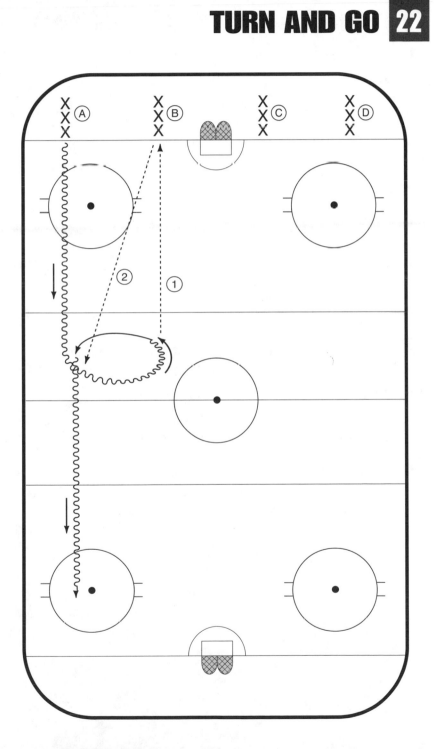

# 23 PIVOT & GO WITH PARTNER

## Purpose

- To practice quick pivots while handling and passing the puck

## Equipment   None

## Time   2-3 minutes

## Procedure

1. Players begin in two equal groups, one at each end of the ice in opposite corners.
2. Partners come from the same line.
3. Players follow the route as shown, making sure to pivot and backward skate with the puck as they prepare to pass.

## Key Points

- Both ends begin the drill on the whistle.
- Players must pivot in a circular fashion, not simply stop and pass.
- Players must accelerate to receive the return pass from the partner.

## Drill Progressions

- Begin the drill skating backward and pivot forward in the turn.
- Increase total number of pivots (add two or three more along the route).
- No gliding allowed; keep feet moving at all times.

# PIVOT & GO WITH PARTNER 23

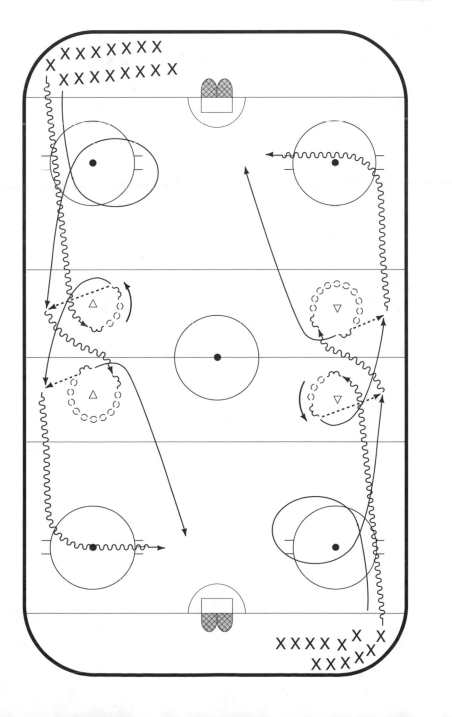

# 24 CENTER PIVOTS

## Purpose

- To maintain puck control off a pass and into situations that require a pivot

## Equipment   None

## Time   2-3 minutes

## Procedure

1. Players begin in four groups, one at each blue line along the boards, creating a half-ice drill.
2. Players skate out with stick blades on the blue line; players from other line pass to the sticks.
3. Players pivot and go, following the route shown.

## Key Points

- Player receiving the pass must have blade of stick on the blue line, keeping body out of neutral zone.
- Turn 180° during pivots.
- Time the pass so that it will be received at the middle of the ice along the blue line.

## Drill Progressions

- Have players drop to their knees out of each pivot and get up as quickly as possible.
- Use skates to kick up the puck at least once during the drill.

# CENTER PIVOTS 24

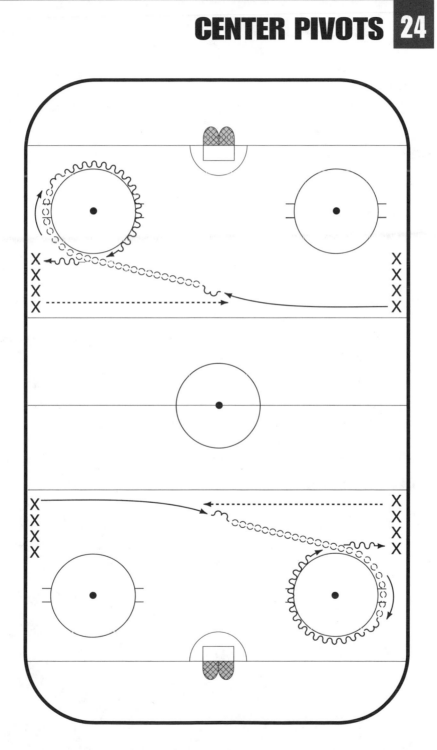

# 25 PARTNER WEAVE

## Purpose

- To use quick passes, followed by hard skating, in order to receive the puck in a give-and-go drill

## Equipment   None

## Time   2 minutes

## Procedure

1. Three pairs of lines work together (six lines total, *A* & *B*, *C* & *D*, *E* & *F*).
2. Once the whistle is blown, the first player from each line skates up ice.
3. After each pass, players accelerate behind their partners and catch up for return pass and possession of the puck.
4. Players handle the puck when it is on their stick, rather than just pushing it along in front.

## Key Points

- Player receiving the pass makes it easier on his partner by angling to the middle of the ice when receiving the pass.
- As players get proficient at this drill, they see that the puck is always in possession and under control.

## Drill Progressions

- Add a second puck.
- Have players attempt drop passing as they cross.

# PARTNER WEAVE 25

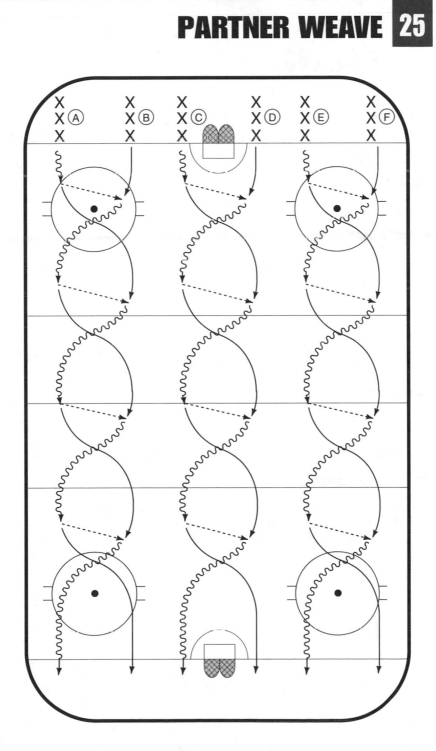

# 26 FORWARD/BACKWARD SKATING

## Purpose

- To practice backward skating as a part of puck control skills development

## Equipment   None

## Time   2 minutes

## Procedure

1. Same as previous six-line drill where two lines work together.
2. One player starts out skating backward as his partner skates forward.
3. Players practice passing the puck, with the player skating backward holding possession while turning 360° or pivoting 180°.
4. Switch roles and skating direction at other end when coming back down the ice.

## Key Points

- Players back pedal with puck and turn while keeping possession.
- This drill simulates a transition play under game conditions and refines puck control skill in both forward and backward positions.

## Drill Progressions

- Have players close their eyes while making pivots.
- Both players must use skates, kicking puck up to stick.
- Players must receive pass in skates instead of on the stick blade.

# FORWARD/BACKWARD SKATING 26

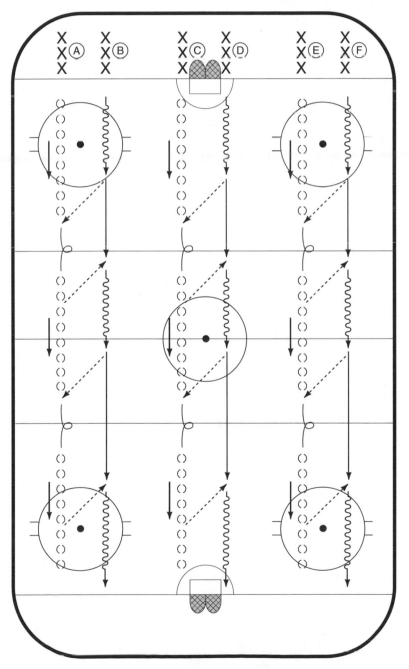

# 27 THREE-PLAYER WEAVE

## Purpose

- To simulate a game attack situation with a line controlling the puck together

## Equipment   None

## Time   2 minutes

## Procedure

1. Players arranged in six lines attempt to weave by threes, following wherever they pass.
2. Once players release the puck, they must cut behind the player who receives it, accelerating to stay together as a unit. Twice up ice, twice back.

## Key Points

- Players must get in a position to receive the pass very quickly after they release the puck (accelerate behind linemates).
- Players should call for the puck.

## Drill Progressions

- Attempt "one time" passes, where the puck does not stop but is always being "bumped" forward.
- Use boards, where applicable, instead of passing directly.
- Try two pucks at once and put puck in skates of each partner, forcing the use of feet as a means of puck control.

# THREE-PLAYER WEAVE 27

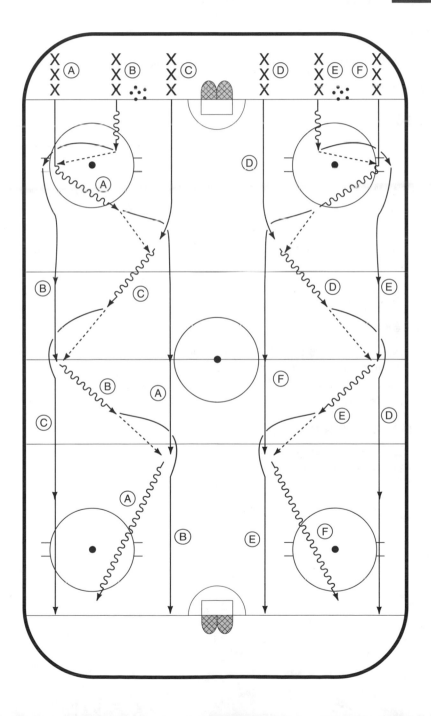

# 28 PUCK CONTROL OVERLOAD

## Purpose

- To practice passing give-and-go by identifying open teammates

## Equipment   None

## Time   4-5 minutes (whistle every 5 seconds)

- Begin full ice, then half ice, then restrict play to one zone only
- 1 minute full ice, 1 minute half ice, 2-3 minutes one zone only

## Procedure

1. Players begin with a partner, with only one partner having a puck. Everyone skates randomly around the ice.
2. On the whistle, players with pucks must identify open partners and give-and-go.
3. Continue passing on each successive whistle; keep feet moving at all times.

## Key Points

- As space is restricted (half ice, then third ice), it becomes more difficult to find an open player and avoid being hit.
- Players should practice pivots, backward skating, and tight turns during this drill.

## Drill Progressions

- Add pylons as obstacles.
- Increase speed, shorten time frame.

# PUCK CONTROL OVERLOAD 28

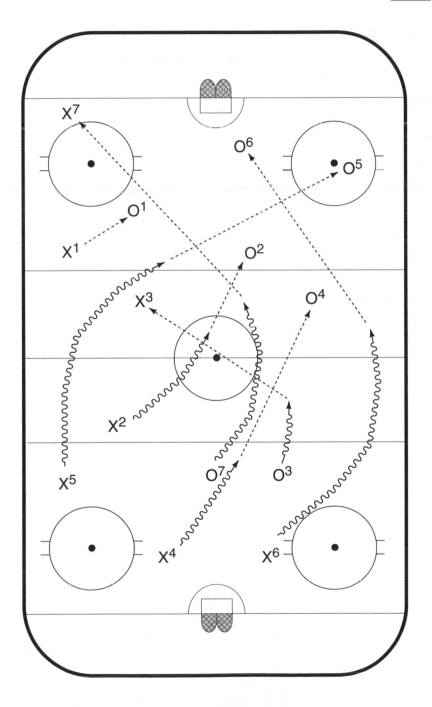

# 29 WALL PASS

## Purpose

- To create puck control situations through quick passes when the puck is against the boards

## Equipment   None

## Time   1-2 minutes

## Procedure

1. Players begin in pairs, one puck between the two.
2. Players roam the ice using quick passes and pivoting as they go.
3. On the whistle, the puck is dumped toward the boards, and the closest partner protects and moves the puck with skates only.
4. On the whistle, puck is passed by kicking to partner who has come up to support.

## Key Points

- Player who is protecting the puck has his hands and stick in the air.
- The partner without the puck positions himself for a quick kick pass.

## Drill Progressions

- Add pressure, with players in a 2-on-2 situation.

# WALL PASS 29

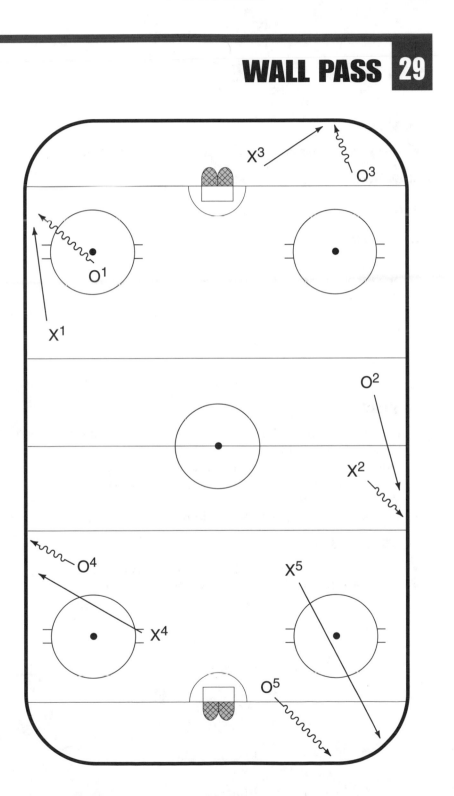

# 30 PASS CONFUSION

## Purpose

- To use quick passing to maintain team puck control

## Equipment   None

## Time   5 minutes

## Procedure

1. Split team into three equal groups and run drill in three zones at one time.
2. Players begin in pairs, with one puck per zone.
3. One pair is "it" and must control the puck for as long as possible in their zone.
4. Those not playing stand on blue line and wait to be called by the leader.
5. When called, players step into the zone and try to retrieve the puck.

## Key Points

- Leader may call for 1-on-2, 2-on-2, 3-on-2, or whatever is needed (discuss before drill).
- On each whistle, one player is added to the unit.
- Players with pucks must go to openings and practice give-and-go to keep possession.
- This is a skill-based activity, so do not allow contact.

## Drill Progressions

- Add a net in each zone and keep score for each pair.
- Build to a three- or four-player possession game.

# PASS CONFUSION 30

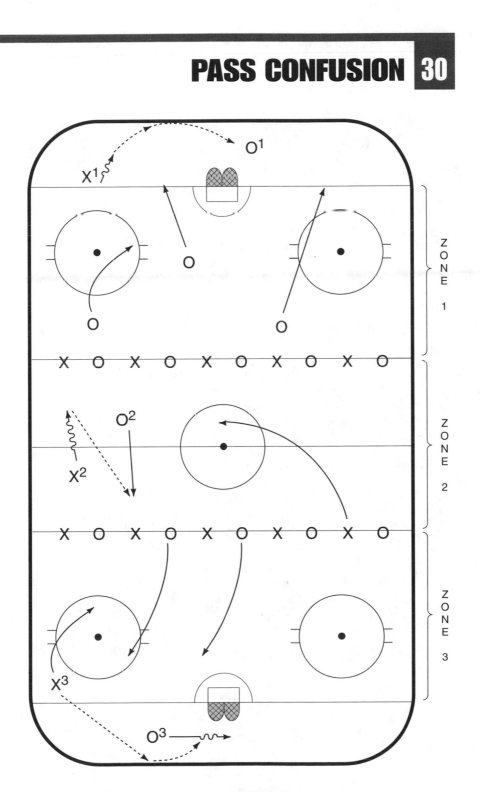

# 5 Pressure: One-on-One Drills

Have you ever heard an athlete described as a "great practice player"? For many athletes success in practice is easy, but often players who show great potential in practice will not succeed at game time because they are not ready for the pressure of a game. This is especially true in the game of hockey, where opponents are constantly trying to restrict time and space in order to force errors. Coaches and players must be aware of this potential problem and use drills to prepare for actual game conditions.

The drills in this chapter force players to control the puck under pressure in basic one-on-one situations. Through practice, you'll be more likely to make good puck control decisions; you'll perform better in games because you'll be more familiar with game conditions.

Begin with the one-on-one activities presented in this chapter. Progress to more difficult pressure situations later in this book to test yourself or your players at a higher level. Remember, the activities described can and should be changed according to your needs. If the drills seem too easy, look at the drill progressions at the end of each drill for ways to make them more challenging.

# 31 FACE THE MUSIC

## Purpose

- To introduce puck control pressure drills in a noncontact situation

## Equipment   None

## Time   20-30 seconds per round

- Five rounds maximum

## Procedure

1. Players begin in pairs.
2. The player with the puck uses a stick while the other cannot.
3. On the whistle, the player with possession tries to control the puck by putting it through the opponent's feet and around his body, while the defending player tries to steal the puck.
4. On the next whistle, players switch roles.

## Key Points

- Players must beat their partner, then immediately turn and face the opponent again.
- Limit partners to a small area of the ice, forcing them to turn without much skating.

## Drill Progressions

- Add contact to the drill.
- Allow both players to use sticks.

# FACE THE MUSIC 31

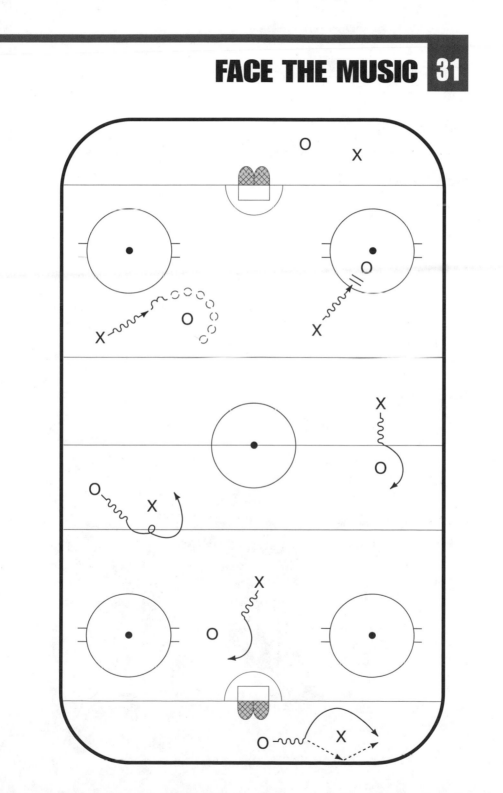

# 32 OFF THE HIP

## Purpose

- To practice using the body as a shield for puck protection

## Equipment   None

## Time   20-30 seconds per round

- Five rounds maximum

## Procedure

1. Players begin in pairs, with one partner having a stick and puck, the other player using only his arms and hands.
2. Player with possession shields his opponent from the puck, keeping him off his hip.
3. Players rotate their bodies in order to fight off opponents and maintain puck control.

## Key Points

- Players should stay in a small area of ice, not doing much skating.
- The player controlling the puck must practice keeping arms extended.

## Drill Progressions

- Have both players use sticks.
- Put players in groups of three. This forces player with puck to rotate from one opponent to the other.

Off the hip

# OFF THE HIP 32

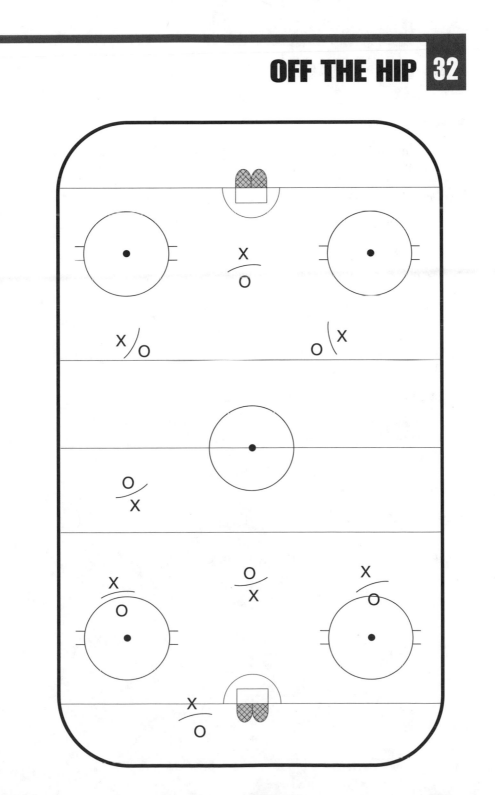

# 33 | WALLPAPER

## Purpose

- To familiarize players with puck control strategies to use while pinned against the boards

## Equipment   None

## Time   20-30 seconds per round

- Five rounds maximum

## Procedure

1. Players go to the boards in pairs; one partner has the puck in his skates while being pinned against the wall. The player with possession has no stick.
2. On the whistle, the opponent must attempt to take the puck away by making contact.

## Key Points

- Players protecting the puck should "make themselves big" by bending their knees and using their arms.
- Players use the boards or glass for balance.
- Players shouldn't stickhandle the puck; instead, they should control the puck with the feet only.

## Drill Progressions

- Have both players use sticks.
- Players must try protecting two pucks at once.

# WALLPAPER 33

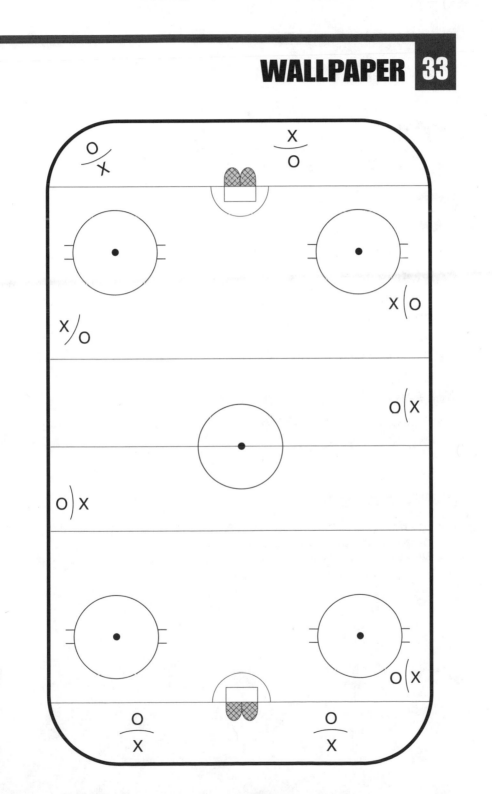

# 34 RABID DOG

## Purpose

- To practice protecting the puck under pressure
- To reinforce second-effort work habits

## Equipment   None

## Time   5 seconds per pair

- 4-5 minutes maximum

## Procedure

1. Players begin in four equal groups, one group at each blue line.
2. On the whistle, the defending players must maintain contact for 5 seconds on the player controlling the puck.
3. Offensive player then goes to the net with the puck, while defender continues checking.

## Key Points

- Player with puck battles to maintain control, with second effort a key to success.
- Players alternate skating from one side of the ice to the other on the whistle.

## Drill Progressions

- Add a second checker to take over from first checker as the play heads to the net.
- Both players must sprint to center ice at the conclusion of the drill, simulating a back-check sequence.

# RABID DOG 34

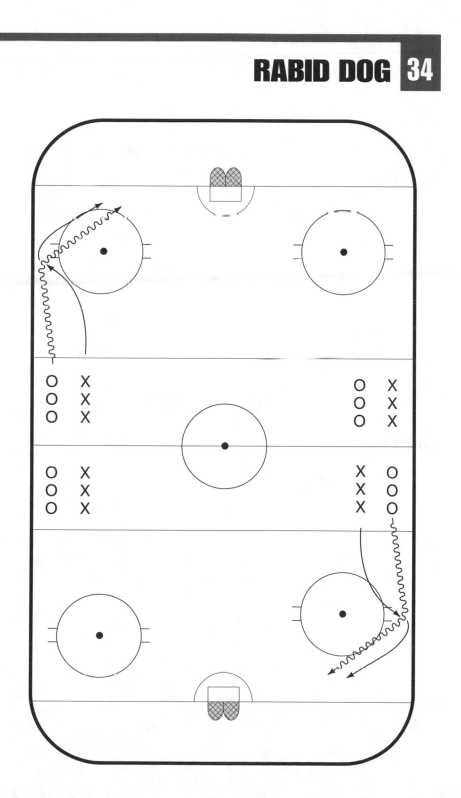

# 35 STUFF THE NET

## Purpose

- To improve quickness and puck control around the net area

## Equipment   None

## Time   20 seconds per pair

## Procedure

1. Drill can be done in three zones if an extra net is put on the ice.
2. On the whistle, player with puck tries to "wrap around" the defender in front.
3. Have 15 to 20 pucks available, so action is nonstop if a puck is put in the net or lost.

## Key Points

- Player behind the net must work on head, shoulder, and arm fakes to get open and away from the defender.
- Defender tries to check the puck by using the stick only.

## Drill Progressions

- Add full body contact by defender.
- Put two defenders in front of the net.

# STUFF THE NET 35

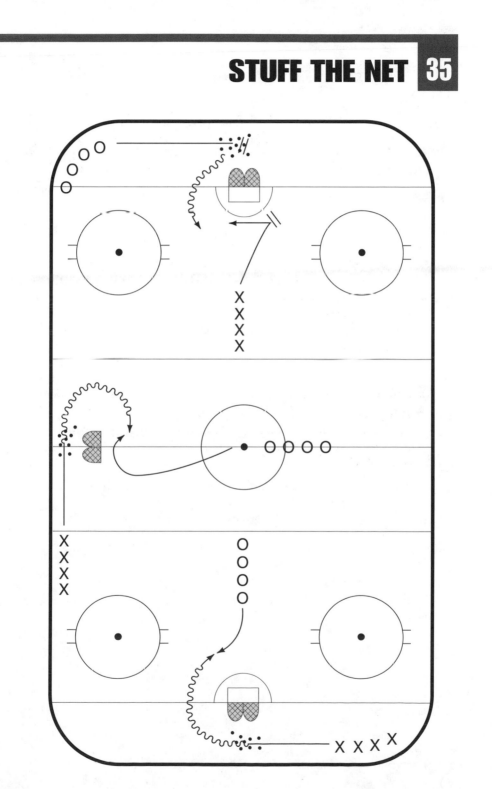

# 36 BLUE LINE DOWN

## Purpose

- To reinforce quickness in puck control during a pressure scoring situation

## Equipment   None

## Time   2-3 minutes

## Procedure

1. Players are paired and split into four even groups at the blue lines.
2. Puck control player must beat defender to the net by quickly responding to the whistle.
3. Defender starts by facing in the opposite direction and must turn to catch attacking player.
4. Alternate sides in each zone.

## Key Points

- The puck carrier is given a one-step lead.
- Remember to force the defender to turn on the drill.

## Drill Progressions

- Start at the blue line face-off dot, then move groups into the corner face-off circles.
- Have players start from knees, stomach, and so on.

# BLUE LINE DOWN 36

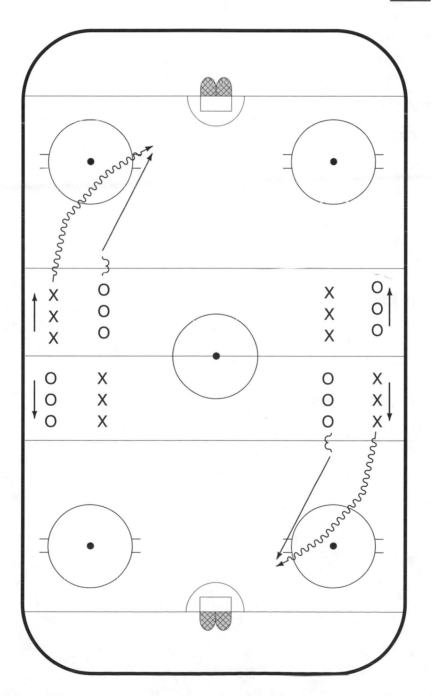

# 37 DOWN THE WALL

## Purpose

- To practice controlling the puck under pressure while attempting to clear the zone

## Equipment   None

## Time   2-3 minutes

## Procedure

1. Players are in two lines on each side of the ice, from the blue line down, facing the end boards.
2. Leader dumps a puck into the corner and players from both lines go for possession.
3. Puck must be skated past the blue line to be considered cleared.
4. Alternate sides in each zone.

## Key Points

- First player to the puck gains possession, while other player tries to strip the puck and carry it out.
- Players should gain possession first, before skating with it; use the boards and the body to protect if necessary.

## Drill Progressions

- Finish the drill with a shot on goal, rather than by clearing.
- Make it a 2-on-1 or 3-on-1 activity.

# DOWN THE WALL 37

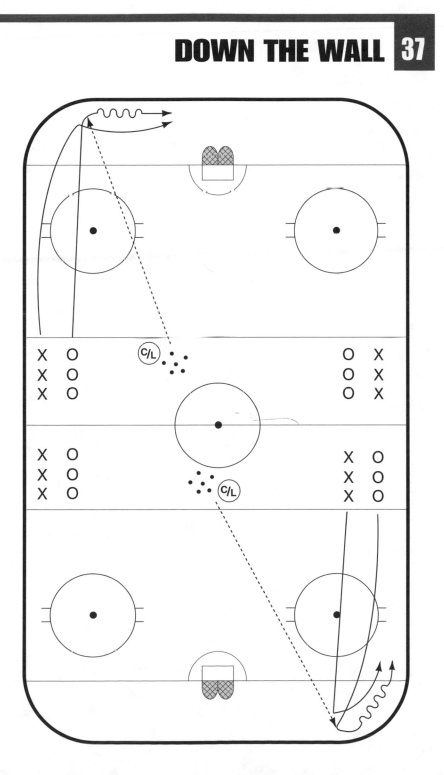

# 38 CIRCLE 1-ON-1

## Purpose

- To condition players
- To practice puck control under pressure

## Equipment   None

## Time   60 seconds per round

## Procedure

1. Ten players drill at once, with one pair of players in each face-off circle. Each player attempts to maintain control in a 1-on-1 situation.
2. Whistle blows every 10 seconds and players rotate to the next circle.
3. After five attempts, players switch partners.

## Key Points

- This is a tiring drill that promotes aerobic conditioning.

## Drill Progressions

- Place three players per circle and turn the drill into a 1-on-2.
- Make the stations 15 seconds instead of 10.

# CIRCLE 1-ON-1 38

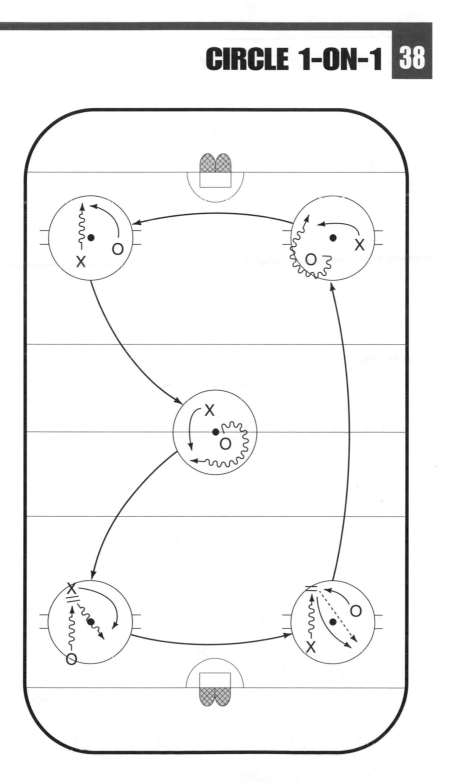

# 39 FULL-ICE 1-ON-1

## Purpose

- To practice full-ice competition for puck control in a 1-on-1 drill

## Equipment    Pylons

## Time    2 minutes per side (4 minutes total)

## Procedure

1. Divide the ice in half lengthwise with pylons.
2. Players from both ends leave on the whistle, making sure to stay on their half of the ice.
3. Players compete for the loose puck passed from the leader and must get to the far goal line in order to score a point.
4. Go from both directions at the same time.

## Key Points

- Players must start at the same time and go around the pylons.
- Leader places the puck anywhere, and players must pursue.

## Drill Progressions

- Add shot at the end of the drill.
- Add second checker who steps in from neutral zone once one player has full possession.

# FULL-ICE 1-ON-1 39

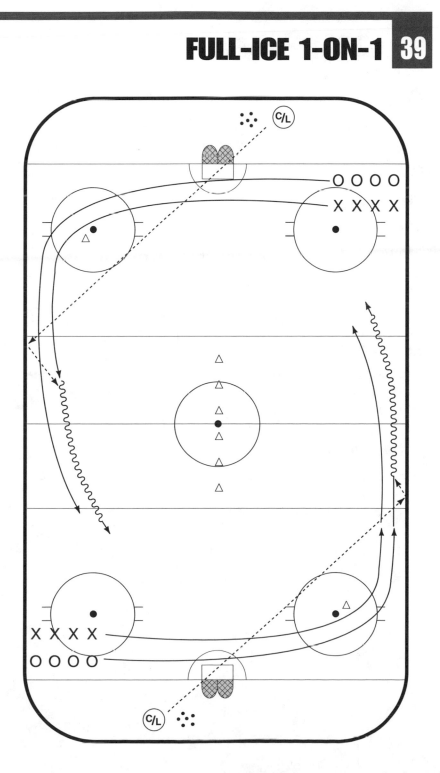

# 40 LOOP 1-ON-1

## Purpose

- To practice straightaway puck control and puck control with pressure when finishing an attack

## Equipment   None

## Time   3-4 minutes

## Procedure

1. Players begin in four equal groups, two at each end.
2. Both ends go on the whistle; player with puck (*A*) goes around net and passes to breaking player (*B*) who goes into other end.
3. The player who initially passed the puck skates to the center red line, turns, and attacks the player coming from the other zone.

## Key Points

- Passing players must skate all the way to the center red line (no cheating).
- Remember to switch sides and go from the other direction.
- Puck carrier tries to beat checker to the goal line.

## Drill Progressions

- Force puck carrier to stay along the boards until the puck is in the other zone.
- Add a shot on the goaltender to finish the drill.

# LOOP 1-ON-1 **40**

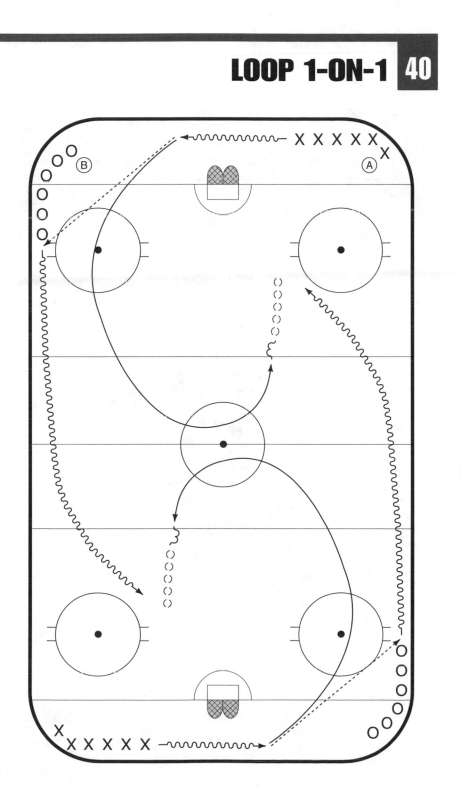

# 6 Puck Control Games

As a player or coach, you know that teams grow tired of the same practice plan day after day. Puck control games are a valuable way to improve skills while making practice more varied and enjoyable.

In puck control games, part or all of the team participates in activities that go beyond an individual working alone in a drill pattern to improve puck control skills. They can be used over the entire ice surface or on a restricted portion of the rink, depending on the objectives you are trying to achieve. In some cases, competition between team members can add to the energy and excitement of a game, while other activities might be more cooperative in nature. Regardless of the drill used, puck control games and activities can be a welcome break from traditional patterns of drilling. Players can continue working on puck control techniques on an individual level, yet enjoy themselves within a small group activity.

The drills in this chapter represent a variety of objectives. Whether your desire is to increase conditioning, work on specific skills, or just have fun, these activities are popular with players of all ages. I have included several unique relay games, as well as a series of three-on-three activities that incorporate puck control and movement. Small group games, such as the three-on-three drills, are an effective way to improve skills and monitor progress. As you try these different activities, be creative and develop your own unique ways of adapting the drills for a particular group of players.

# 41 TORPEDOES

## Purpose

- To practice puck control and puck protection while being "hunted"

## Equipment   As many pylons as possible

## Time   30 seconds per round

- Approximately 5 minutes

## Procedure

1. Leaders (hunters) are "armed" with small torpedoes (pylons) on the end of their sticks.
2. On the whistle, players come from one end with a puck and try to get to the other end without being hit by a hunter's torpedo.
3. Players must control puck from end-to-end.

## Key Points

- Once a player is hit, he joins the hunters and shoots torpedoes.
- Continue going end-to-end until only one player remains.

## Drill Progressions

- Start all players in the neutral zone, with hunters on either side.
- Players with puck can go to either end boards.

# TORPEDOES 41

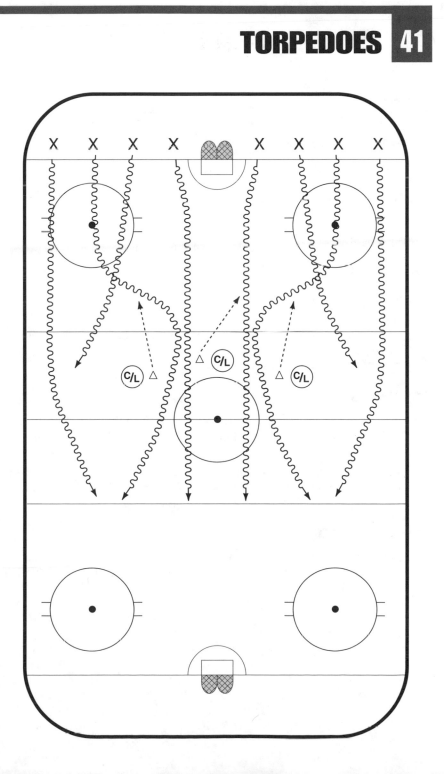

# 42 MONKEY IN THE MIDDLE

## Purpose

- To practice relaxing while controlling the puck and making good decisions when pressured

## Equipment   None

## Time   4-5 minutes

## Procedure

1. Split team into four or five equal groups.
2. Teams form a circle anywhere on the ice, then send one member to another group to act as the "monkey."
3. The monkey, in the center of the circle, attempts to gain control of the puck by intercepting a pass.
4. The circle scores one point for each successful pass around the monkey while keeping possession of the puck.
5. Players count out loud each time a point is scored.

## Key Points

- After five rounds (with a different monkey each time, changing on the whistle) points are totaled to see which circle scored the most points.
- Players in the circle can score double points by faking out the monkey or by maintaining possession if attacked. Developing hand-foot puck control skills is the key focus.

## Drill Progressions

- Add another puck to each circle.
- Combine groups and have two large circles with two monkeys in the middle.

# MONKEY IN THE MIDDLE 42

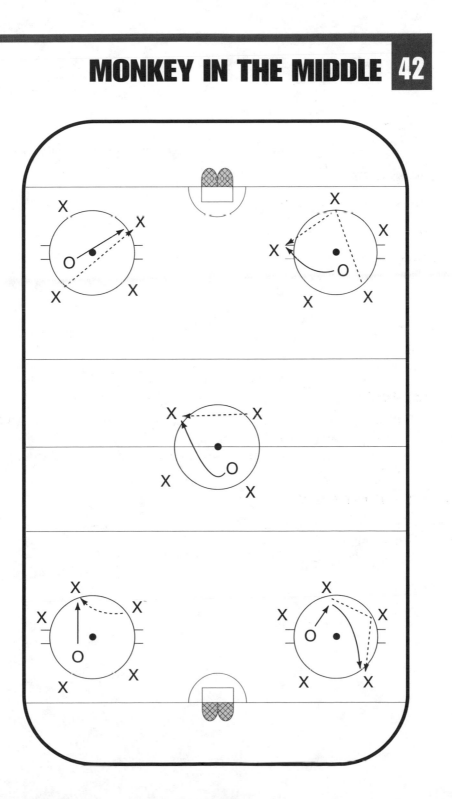

# 43 CIRCLE RELAY

## Purpose

- To practice puck control at high speed in a competitive situation

## Equipment   None

## Time   1.5-2 minutes per set

- Five rounds maximum

## Procedure

1. Split team in two equal groups and have one at either end zone face-off circle.
2. On the whistle, players begin by circling closest circle once, then skate down ice and hand puck off to person in front of line at other end.
3. Players go to the back of the line that they just passed to.

## Key Points

- This is a simple relay that forces players to handle the puck while turning at high speed.
- Players cannot move until the puck is handed off to them—no long-distance passes!

## Drill Progressions

- Start the drill by circling backward, then pivot to skate forward to the other end.
- Start both ends at the same time with two pucks.

# CIRCLE RELAY 43

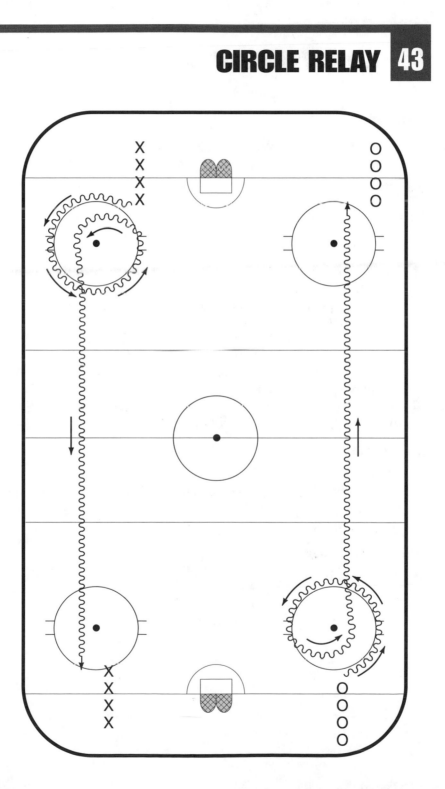

# 44 CONDITIONING RELAY

## Purpose

- To enhance puck control skills while improving "sprint conditioning"

## Equipment   None

## Time   4-5 minutes per set

## Procedure

1. Divide team in half, then divide each half into three or four groups of equal numbers.
2. Place four pucks on the goal line for each group, with groups at the blue line facing the end boards.
3. On the whistle, players must retrieve a puck from the goal line and place it on the blue line, then repeat for the remaining three pucks (all four pucks will be retrieved and brought to the blue line where the player began the drill).
4. Once two pucks are retrieved, the next person in the group begins by replacing them on the goal line.

## Key Points

- Players must deposit puck on the line(s), not pass and go.
- The number of groups used depends on the number of players participating in the activity (three or four players is an ideal number per group).

## Drill Progressions

- Go full ice. Have players skate from goal line to goal line in a similar procedure.

# CONDITIONING RELAY 44

# 45  LINE RELAY

## Purpose

- To promote puck control skills through competitive relay activities

## Equipment    None

## Time

- Usually 60 to 90 seconds per set, with smaller numbers of players taking less time to complete the set

## Procedure

1. Divide team in half, with teams on both blue lines spread apart by a stick length.
2. Player at front of line begins by skating hard around the net, then weaves between teammates on the blue line until back to original position.
3. The player fires the puck around the boards to next player who comes from the other direction.

## Key Points

- Have players move back one space in the line once they complete their circuit, so a new participant is ready to receive the puck.
- Players should keep sticks tight to the body when acting as a pylon.

## Drill Progressions

- Try this drill skating backward.
- Use two pucks at once, going from both directions, keeping the head up.

# LINE RELAY 45

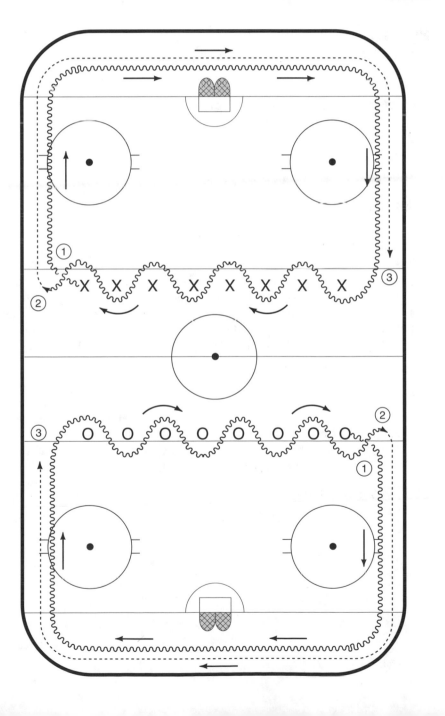

# 46 SADLER DOUBLE BARREL

## Purpose

- To practice puck control in extreme situations using the body as a shield

## Equipment    Six pylons, lots of pucks

## Time

- Depends on size of group and skill level
- Usually 30-40 seconds per player

## Procedure

1. Team is split into two equal groups, one on either blue line, spaced a stick-length apart.
2. Player skates with puck around the net to the face-off circle, pivots, and skates backward to the other face-off circle.
3. Player must control puck while players on blue line shoot pucks and try to knock the puck off the stick of the puck carrier.
4. On second time through, player must skate between blue line and pylons, while the other players interfere with the stick, gloves, and body of puck carrier.

## Key Points

- Players should not attempt to raise the puck and hit the puck carrier in the first part of the drill.
- On the second pass, players should attempt to hit puck carrier's elbows and hands to dislodge the puck.

## Drill Progressions

- Use a trailer (checker) who is constantly on the puck carrier's heels.

# SADLER DOUBLE BARREL 46

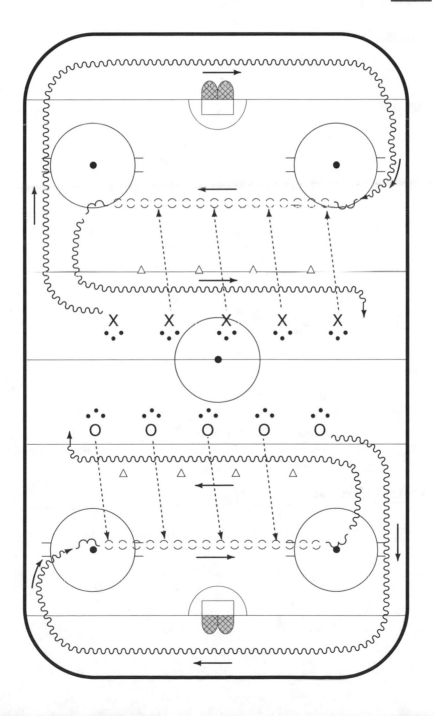

# 47 3-ON-3 END ZONE

## Purpose

- To refine puck control skills in a confined space under extreme pressure

**Equipment**    If done as a half-ice drill, two extra nets are required.

**Time**    20 seconds per group

- 3-4 minutes maximum

## Procedure

1. Split team in half with each group at either end of the ice lined up single file at the face-off dot near the blue line.
2. Nets are placed across from each other in the zone.
3. Leader dumps a puck; the first three players from each line start playing 3-on-3.
4. The group of three that retrieves the puck becomes the offensive group, the other the defensive. All three offensive players must touch the puck before a goal is counted.
5. No contact is allowed.

## Key Points

- 20-second shifts make for a high-speed and fun activity.
- On the whistle, puck is left for next group of players, and all six should vacate the zone at high speed.
- If the puck in play leaves the zone, the leader puts another back in and play continues.

## Drill Progressions

- Add full body contact.
- Make the drill a 3-on-2 or 4-on-3, switching at leader's discretion.

# 3-ON-3 END ZONE 47

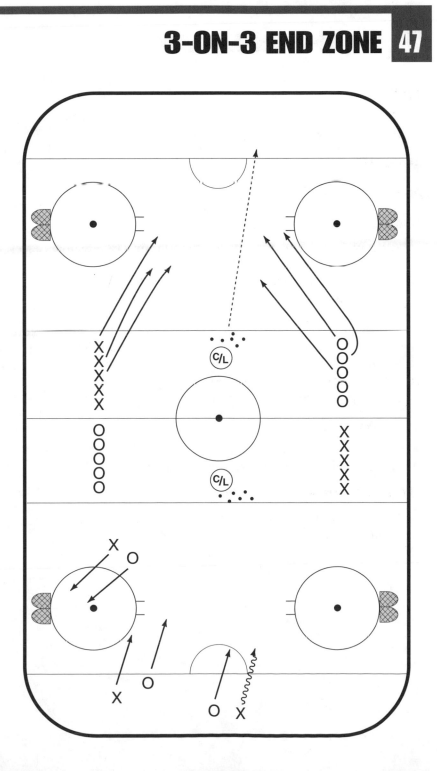

# 48 3-ON-3 GOAL LINE

## Purpose

- To practice puck control in offensive situations while driving to the goal line and net

## Equipment  None

## Time  1-2 minutes per set

## Procedure

1. All players are seated on the bench, split into two teams.
2. Pucks are placed in the center circle.
3. On the whistle, three players from each team jump the boards, with one player from each group of three gaining possession of a puck.
4. The three players on each side must all touch the puck before a shot can be taken, with one player carrying the puck to the goal line.
5. When a goal is scored, all three exit the zone and get another puck. Repeat the process until all three have scored.

## Key Points

- First team with three goals gets one point.
- No offsides allowed when clearing and reentering the zone.

## Drill Progressions

- Put a time limit on each group, varying the amount of time from group to group.

# 3-ON-3 GOAL LINE 48

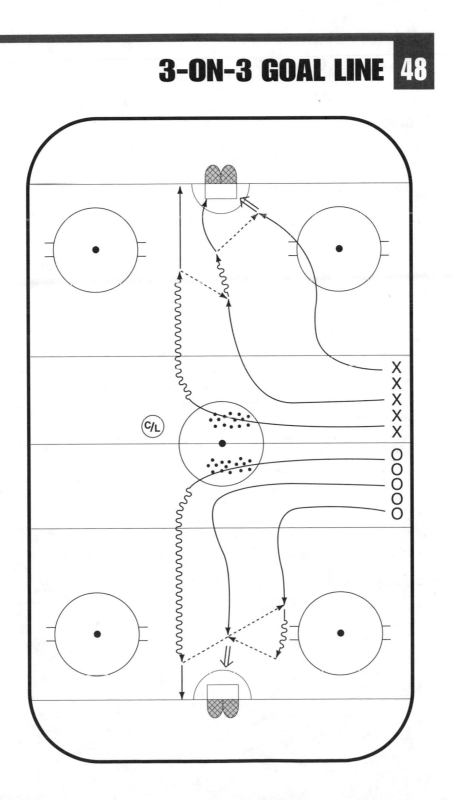

# 49 3-ON-3 CENTER ZONE

## Purpose

- To add variety to puck control work in an unusual and competitive environment

## Equipment   None

## Time

- Continuous for 3-4 minutes
- 20-30 seconds per shift, then rotate new players into the activity

## Procedure

1. Put nets back-to-back in center circle, with two equal teams, one on either blue line.
2. Team from one blue line attacks one of the nets; the other team attacks the opposite goalie. Each team actively tries to retrieve the puck when the opposition has control.
3. Players rotate left to right along their respective blue lines, with three new players in the game whenever the whistle blows.
4. Players on blue lines can help their teammates when the puck goes astray by putting it back in play.
5. If puck leaves neutral zone area, leader puts another puck into play.

## Key Points

- Gives goalies work on looking behind for puck, as well as in front.
- Players must use "ice vision" in order to spot open teammates.

## Drill Progressions

- Go to a 4-on-4 situation.
- Move the two lines closer together, leaving less space for players to maneuver.

# 3-ON-3 CENTER ZONE 49

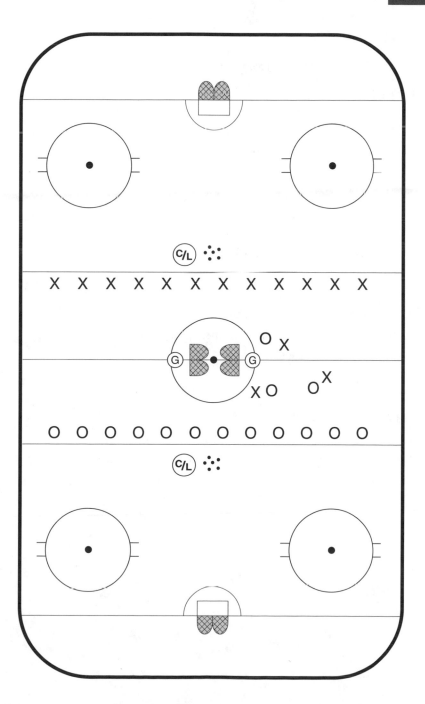

# 50 TIRE SHINNY

## Purpose

- To work on puck control skills under controlled conditions

## Equipment    Four tires

## Time    5-7 minutes

- 30-second rest breaks every 45 seconds

## Procedure

1. Put one tire at each face-off dot outside the two blue lines.
2. All players are active with right wingers and left wingers staying in their "lanes" in the neutral zone (imagine a line drawn between the two tires; see diagram).
3. Centers and defense only can go through the middle of the ice.
4. Players play a regular game.

## Key Points

- Any winger going into the mid-ice area is penalized and must go off for two minutes.
- The tires help prevent the entire team going to the puck all the time, developing awareness of zones and positions.

## Drill Progressions

- Add another player or two for each team (6-on-6, 7-on-7).
- Try two pucks. Players, remember to keep heads up!

# TIRE SHINNY 50

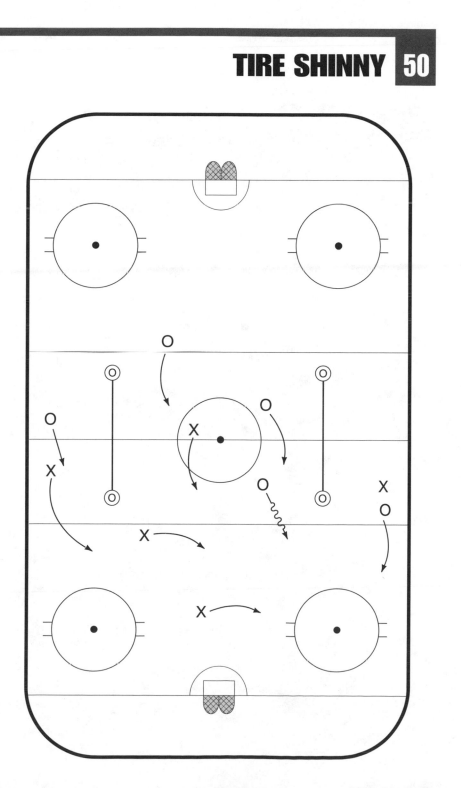

# 7 Game Situation Drills

The activities in this chapter simulate game situations that force players to use puck control and thinking skills. All of the drills involve some form of pressure—either restricted time or space, in even-strength or outmanned situations. In many instances, the drills will force players to perform and make judgments at higher speeds than they may be accustomed to; players will learn to handle the complications that pressure creates. These drills may seem difficult or confusing at first to younger or less-skilled players; however, once you are able to complete these drills properly, your chances of being successful in actual games will be greatly improved.

The drills in this chapter begin with isolated situations, such as a two-on-one, and center around "segments" of play: two-on-two, three-on-three, and so on. They progress to full five-on-five activities that closely simulate actual games. This approach provides insight into how you can apply puck control skills first on a simple level, then in more demanding game conditions. As is always the case, to prevent confusion, frustration, and failure, begin simply and build progressively to more difficult tasks as players demonstrate the necessary puck control and thinking skills required to complete the more complex drills in this chapter. To get the most out of game situation drills, resist the temptation to go directly to the most challenging activities and pay close attention to the instructions for the activities.

# 51 2-ON-1 ATTACK

## Purpose

- To force the puck carrier to make good puck control decisions

## Equipment   None

## Time   3-5 minutes

## Procedure

1. Leader has pucks at center and will pass to a player on either side of the ice in a half-ice drill.
2. Three players skate from the goal line toward the red line with two players on offense and the center player on defense.
3. The defensive player attacks the side that the puck goes to.
4. Puck carrier can either attempt to outmaneuver attacker or make a good pass to partner.

## Key Points

- Defensive forward skates to the blue line, while the two offensive players skate all the way to the red line.

## Drill Progressions

- Have defensive player fake his coverage, allowing the puck carrier to control the puck and attack.
- Add a second defender after the leader passes to either side.

# 2-ON-1 ATTACK 51

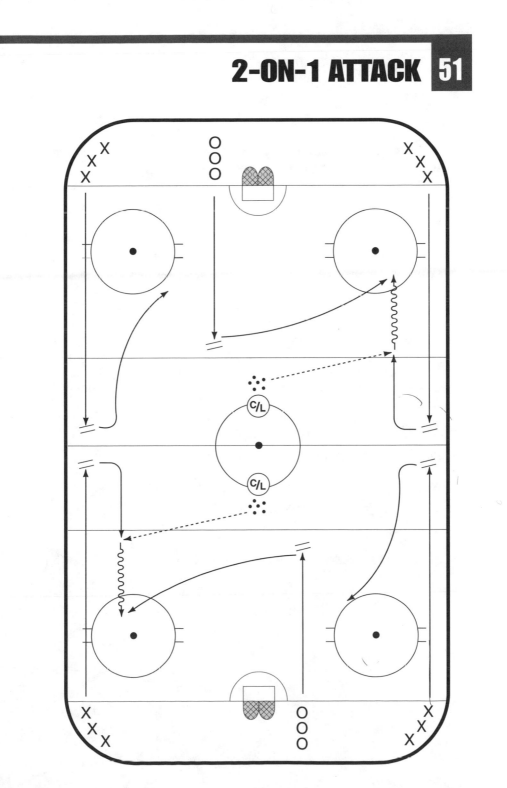

# 52 2-ON-2 LOW

## Purpose

- To force players to improve puck control skills and decision making in a confined space under pressure

## Equipment   None

## Time   5-7 minutes

- 15-20 seconds per set

## Procedure

1. Two players are on offense, two on defense, playing below the hash marks in either zone, creating a half-ice drill.
2. The two offensive players take their positions. When the leader dumps puck to either offensive player, the two defensive players attack, while the offensive players attempt to maintain possession.
3. Once the drill is completed, the next group is sent into the other corner and the drill is repeated.

## Key Points

- Players must develop essential puck control skills to avoid defenders.
- Play stops when the puck is smothered by the goaltender, put in the net by the offensive pair, or cleared past the hash marks.

## Drill Progressions

- Add one player on offense to make it a 3-on-2, increasing offensive options.
- Add one player on defense to make it a 2-on-3, increasing the pressure on the offensive players.

# 2-ON-2 LOW 52

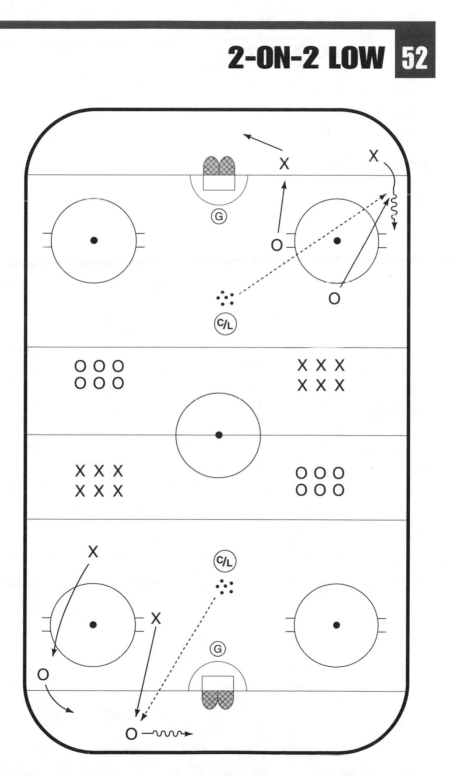

# 53 3-ON-3 ALL BACK

## Purpose

- To maintain puck control while gaining the offensive zone

## Equipment   None

## Time   3-5 minutes

## Procedure

1. First three players come down the ice to receive a pass from leader and attempt to score at that end.
2. At the same time, next three players start skating backward to the blue line, pivot, and skate forward to the next blue line.
3. After the first shot, the leader passes a second puck to the offensive group of three and they attempt to maintain possession of the puck against the opposing three players. The offense completes the drill by shooting on the goalie at the same end of the rink they started from.

## Key Points

- Defenders must stop at the second blue line and cannot attack beyond that point.
- Do not allow dumping of the puck into the offensive zone.
- If the neutral zone is clogged, encourage players to regroup, go back to the zone where the attack began, and try again.

## Drill Progressions

- Vary the situation, one time sending only two defenders, next time sending four.
- Allow defenders to attack beyond the blue line.

# 3-ON-3 ALL BACK 53

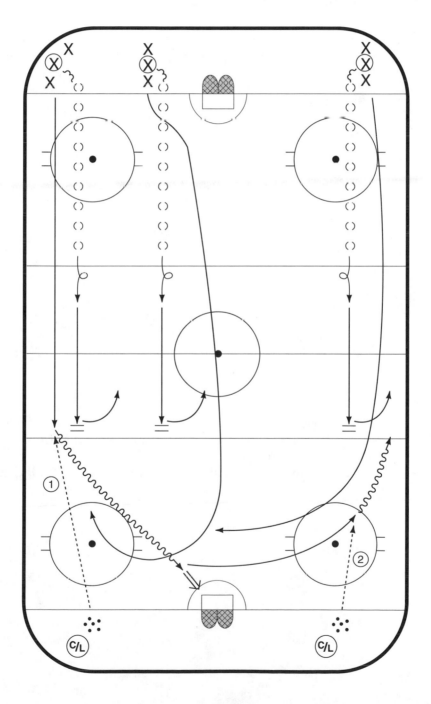

# 54 WEBBIE CYCLE

## Purpose

- To practice puck control in the offensive zone by using teammates and boards

## Equipment   None

## Time   10 seconds maximum per line

## Procedure

1. Groups of three at both ends; use alternate corners.
2. Leader dumps a puck into a corner and three players attempt to cycle by back passing along the boards.
3. Players stay spread apart and continue to cycle until, at the players' discretion, one comes across and shoots or passes for scoring play.

## Key Points

- The puck always goes into the corner, while players cycle in the other direction, up the boards toward the blue line.
- Players should learn how to dump "softly," making it easier for teammates to handle the puck.

## Drill Progressions

- Add one defensive player to challenge in different areas of the cycle. Offensive players must "read and react" and should not make a pass that will be intercepted.
- Add a weak side defensive player who jumps into the play at leader's signal.

# WEBBIE CYCLE 54

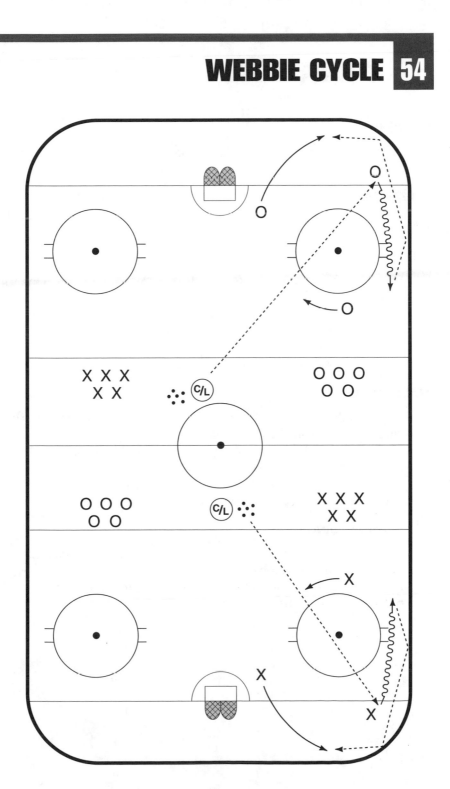

# 55 3-ON-3 LOW

## Purpose

- To practice puck control skills in the offensive zone under pressure

## Equipment   None

## Time   30 seconds per round

## Procedure

1. Play must occur below the tops of the face-off circles or hash marks (leader's discretion).
2. Three offensive players position themselves anywhere in the zone, while the three defensive players must begin the drill lying on their stomachs in front of the net.
3. Play begins when leader blows the whistle.

## Key Points

- A good follow-up to the "Webbie Cycle" drill (#54), only with pressure. It's also a progression from the "2-on-2 Low" drill (#52).
- The defensive threesome should have two defensemen and one forward; however, any combination of three is acceptable.
- Offensive players must attempt quick 1-on-1 puck control maneuvers and short, accurate passing to get a shot on goal.

## Drill Progressions

- Defensive players must play without sticks or turn sticks upside down, placing the knob of the stick on the ice.
- Add an offensive defenseman who jumps into the play at the signal, making it a confined 4-on-3.

# 3-ON-3 LOW 55

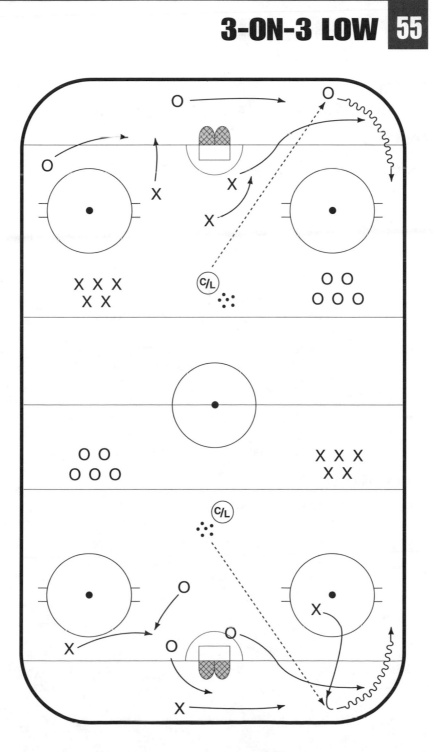

# 56 5-ON-2 FULL ICE

## Purpose

- To build offensive players' confidence in their puck control skills

## Equipment   None

## Time   4-5 minutes, continuously

- 30-45 seconds per round

## Procedure

1. Two teams position themselves as shown.
2. Five players rush on two defensemen, gain control of the offensive zone, then work for their best scoring opportunity.
3. Once puck is in the net, saved by the goalie, or exits the zone, the two defensemen under attack get a puck and start out 5-on-2 in the other direction.
4. The original three offensive players remain in the zone and wait for their next rush while the play goes to the other end.

## Key Points

- Continuous drill forces players to be ready at both ends once whistle is blown.
- Plays should be at game speed, simulating actual conditions.

## Drill Progressions

- Add another puck and another offensive player.
- Turn the drill into a 5-on-3, 6-on-3, 6-on-4, or other configurations.

# 5-ON-2 FULL ICE 56

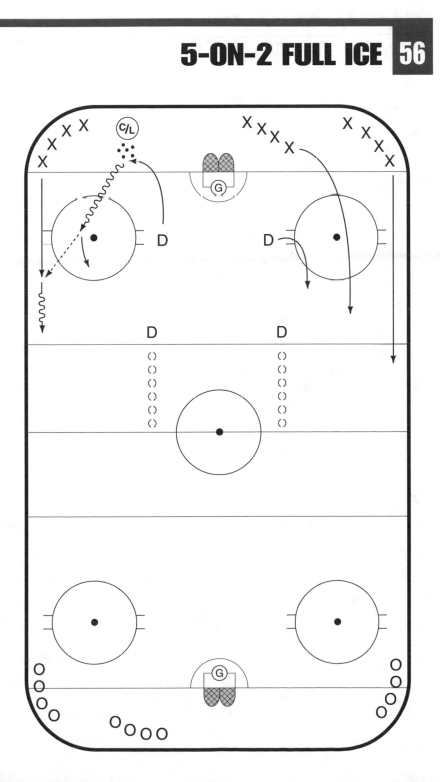

# 57 POWER PLAY CHALLENGE

## Purpose

- To create a power play situation, emphasizing puck control into the opponents' zone

## Equipment   None

## Time   Approximately 5-7 minutes

- Three turns on power play
- Three turns penalty killing

## Procedure

1. Team is split in two and lined up along their respective boards in the neutral zone with one group starting the power play, the other group penalty killing.
2. Power play team has three chances to score, using a new puck for each opportunity and earning a point each time they score.
3. Penalty killers earn a point each time they clear the puck beyond their blue line.
4. Play begins when leader dumps puck into power play end of the ice.
5. Once the three chances are used, switch offensive and defensive roles.

## Key Points

- Do not allow penalty killers to "press"; they must stay behind the center red line.
- Start out at three times each and expand to five, depending on how quickly the drill progresses.

## Drill Progressions

- Allow penalty killers to attack immediately when puck is dumped in.
- Allow power play group to "pull the goalie" for an extra attacker.

# POWER PLAY CHALLENGE 57

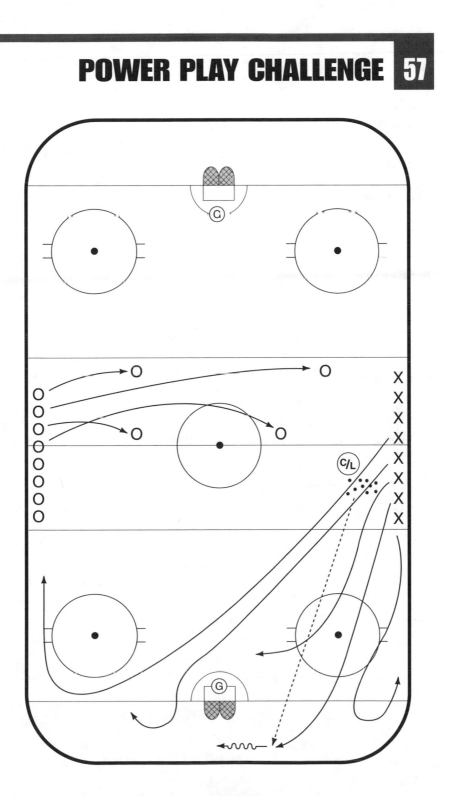

## 58 KNOB 5-ON-5

### Purpose

- To maintain puck control by making good decisions while playing with an advantage

### Equipment   None

### Time   3-4 minutes

- 30 seconds per set

### Procedure

1. Defensive team must play with the knob of the stick on the ice.
2. Offensive players attempt to maintain control of the puck in the zone by quick maneuvering and passing in a half-ice drill.
3. Once the puck exits zone, begin new sequence.

### Key Points

- Because of their disadvantage, defensive players will want to make contact. Offensive players must be patient and maintain control of the puck, by controlling the puck with their skates or by passing the puck to an open teammate.

### Drill Progressions

- Go full ice, forcing offensive team to gain the offensive zone through puck possession.

# KNOB 5-ON-5 58

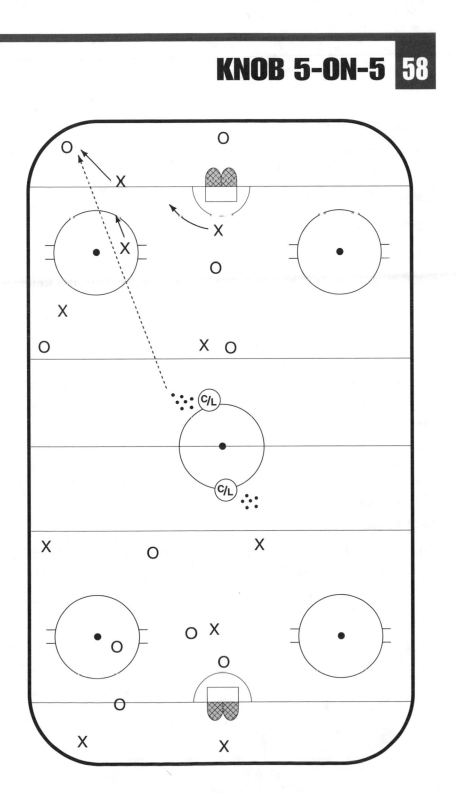

# 59 5-ON-5 BREAKOUT

## Purpose

- To simulate game situations in breaking out of the defensive zone, using puck control skills to gain the offensive zone

## Equipment   None

## Time   7-10 minutes

## Procedure

1. Divide players into two teams. Divide each group into units of five. Both teams begin on their respective benches.
2. Leader selects one unit of five from each team and dumps a puck into either defensive zone.
3. Players must go to their breakout positions and attempt to gain the offensive zone of the other team.
4. Award points for successfully clearing defensive zone, gaining offensive zone, and scoring goals.

## Key Points

- Similar to the "Power Play Challenge" drill (#57); however, allow the checking team to apply full pressure.
- Keep a running total of points, with a maximum of three points per rush.

## Drill Progressions

- Teams can attempt variations of breakout drills, such as wingers off the boards, defensemen jumping up as fourth forward, and so on.

# 5-ON-5 BREAKOUT 59

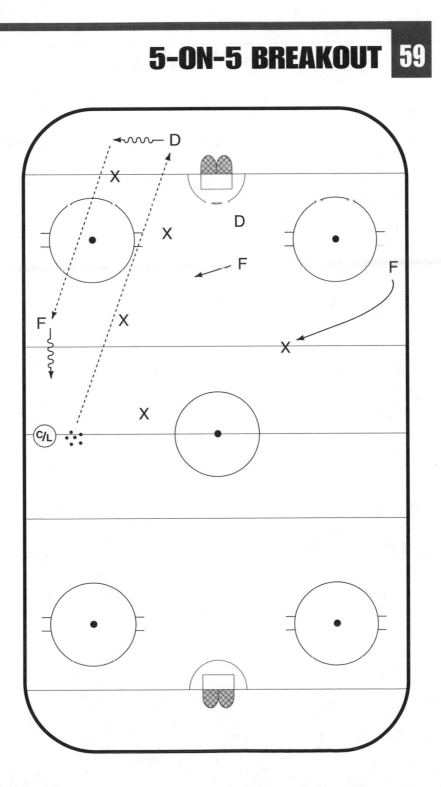

# 60 5-ON-5 SITUATION DRILL

## Purpose

- To practice and reinforce judging situations both offensively and defensively
- To use puck control to gain an advantage on the attack

## Equipment   None

## Time   8-10 minutes

## Procedure

1. Defensemen are sitting together on one bench.
2. All forwards are in one end of the ice, grouped according to their lines with defensive forwards in the face-off circle.
3. Two defensemen skate out to the blue line from the bench, and two more go down to the goal area.
4. Before the puck is put into play, leader tells defensive players when to start back-checking. Stagger defensive players' releases.
5. One unit of five goes full ice and attempts to score, knowing that the defensive forwards are on their way.

## Key Points

- Lines should be in different colors, with defensemen having their own color as well.
- This is a drill that helps defensive players learn coverage in their own end.

## Drill Progressions

- Use only one or two back-checkers to give the offense an advantage.
- Start the defensive forwards outside the blue line to practice different back-check patterns such as 1-2-2, trap, and so on.

# 5-ON-5 SITUATION DRILL 60

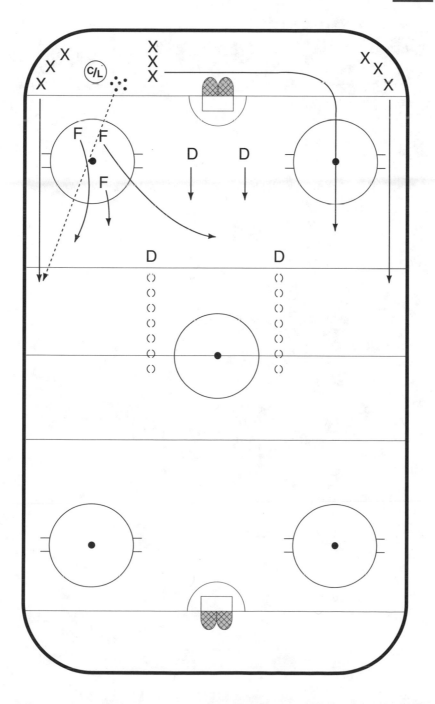

# 8 Speed Drills

In hockey, nothing strikes more fear in your opponent than your ability to control the puck while attacking at high speed. An old hockey adage says, "A *great* move executed at average speed becomes a *good* move, while a *good* move executed at high speed becomes a *great* move!" Speed—in virtually all sports, at all positions—can be the difference between success and failure; you should reinforce this aspect of hockey in practice.

In the same way a cornerback in football must grant a "cushion" to a wide receiver with blazing speed and good hands to avoid getting burned by a long touchdown pass, so too must hockey defenders give the short gain to speed skaters in order to defend against the "long bomb." This cushion presents tremendous offensive opportunities.

The drills in this chapter force players to practice puck control skills at high speed. In challenging yourself to go "flat out" in drills, you will be pushing the limits of your puck control skills, increasing your ability to exploit weaknesses in your opponents. While you can adapt these drills for almost all levels of play, players should have attained some basic puck control skills before attempting them. However, the sooner you are able to combine puck handling skills with speed, the sooner you will be able dominate and more fully enjoy this aspect of the game.

# 61 FULL THROTTLE

## Purpose

- To practice maintaining puck control at a very high speed, moving legs continuously

## Equipment   Six pylons

## Time   4-5 minutes total

## Procedure

1. Split team into two equal groups with players on opposite sides of the ice at the red lines.
2. Both groups begin activity on the whistle and follow the path as diagrammed, with players picking up pucks at the blue line.
3. At the end of the route, players shoot on goal.

## Key Points

- Players must gain speed out of each turn by "pumping" the legs— no gliding allowed.
- Move the pylons and skate in the opposite direction following the same route

## Drill Progressions

- Make the turns tighter between pylons, forcing players out of their comfort zone.
- Add a back-checker who harasses the puck carrier throughout the drill.

# FULL THROTTLE  61

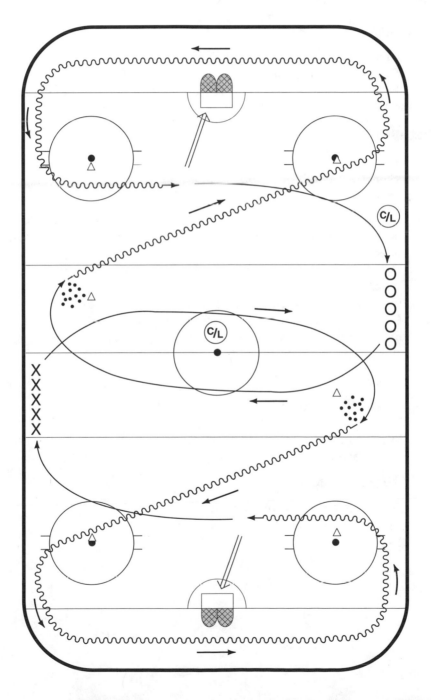

# 62 SPEED DEMON 1-ON-1

## Purpose

- To assess foot speed of defensemen
- To assess offensive speed and puck control of player with puck
- To develop an offensive player's ability to judge the foot speed of his opponent

## Equipment   None

## Time   5-6 minutes

## Procedure

1. Forwards are in two equal groups, one at each end of the ice in opposite corners. Defensemen are in the center face-off circle, with one going to each end to start the drill.
2. Drill begins on the whistle and starts from both ends at the same time.
3. Defensemen cannot move until the forward touches the puck.
4. Vary the drill by putting the puck farther away from the net, making it tougher for defensemen to catch the forward. (See numbered starting puck positions on diagram.)

## Key Points

- Defensemen must skate backward until they reach the nearest blue line.
- Provides a good assessment tool, especially the second effort by both players.

## Drill Progressions

- Send two forwards and make it a "desperate" 2-on-1.
- Add a checker to harass the puck carrier.

# SPEED DEMON 1-ON-1 62

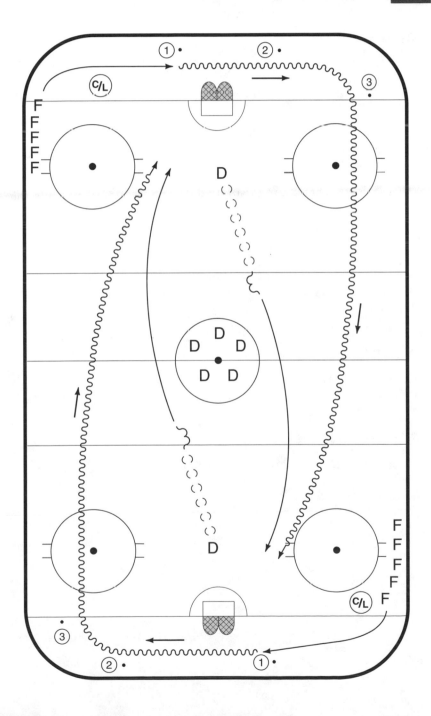

# 63 HOYER 2-ON-2

## Purpose

- To practice puck control at high speed while attacking the opposing team

## Equipment   None

## Time   3-4 minutes

## Procedure

1. Groups of players are positioned at each corner of the rink with pucks.
2. Play begins on the whistle at one end (bottom of diagram), and a loop 1-on-1 is attempted (*A*).
3. On next whistle, loop 1-on-1 starts at the other end, with the previous two players coming down ice to make it a 2-on-2 (*B*).
4. Player on offense in first part of drill must be a defensive player in second part.
5. Next whistle, repeat pattern.

## Key Points

- Should be done at high speed.
- Verbal communication is vital to help players learn to identify who their partner is.

## Drill Progressions

- Use the same procedure to turn this into a 3-on-3.

# HOYER 2-ON-2 63

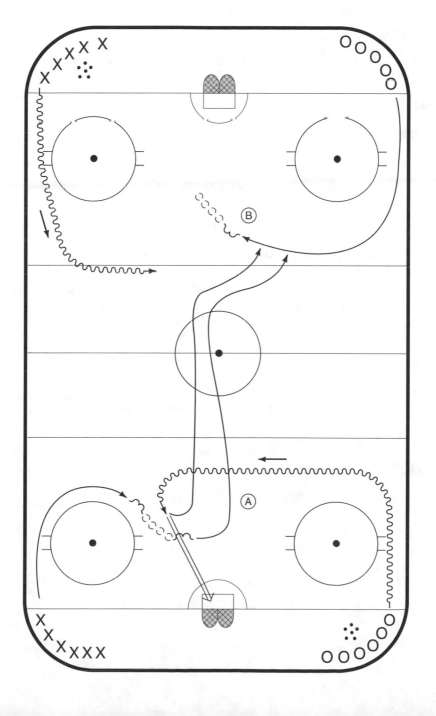

# 64 FOUR-LINE RUSHES

## Purpose

- To create puck control situations at high speed while simulating game conditions

## Equipment   None

## Time   40-60 seconds

## Procedure

1. Defensemen start on the players' bench, ready to jump into the play as required.
2. One line starts by going full ice, 3-on-0, with no puck (top of diagram).
3. Players loop and receive a pass from leader *A* and skate 3-on-0 the other way.
4. After a shot, leader *B* passes another puck and one defenseman joins in from the bench, creating a 3-on-1 situation.
5. Leader *A* passes again; two defensemen jump in, skating 3-on-2 down the ice.

## Key Points

- Once the line turns to finish with a 3-on-2, the next line jumps in from the opposite end to begin the cycle again, going 3-on-0 without a puck.
- High speed is critical.

## Drill Progressions

- Add back-checkers to the final two parts of the drill.

# FOUR-LINE RUSHES 64

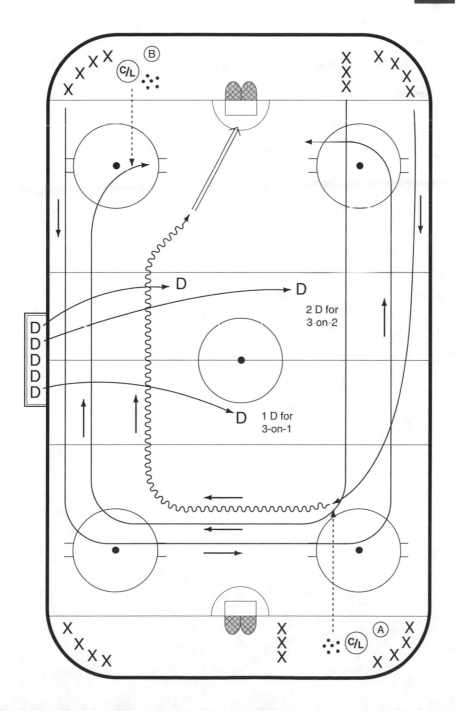

2 D for
3 on-2

1 D for
3-on-1

# 65 KILLER'S GOALIE BUMP

## Purpose

- To practice puck control for goalies and team transition to offense

## Equipment   None

## Time   3-4 minutes

## Procedure

1. Drill will start from one end, then the other.
2. All players must jump from the bench as puck is dumped on net.
3. Goalie controls puck and then passes to designated area at the red line where a forward is waiting.
4. Play a 5-on-0 to finish the drill.

## Key Points

- Player taking the pass must stay onside at red line.
- Next group will receive pass from the other goalie.
- Try to move the puck up ice as quickly as possible.

## Drill Progressions

- Add two defensemen and one forward to make the drill a 5-on-3.
- Go two full units (5-on-5).

# KILLER'S GOALIE BUMP 65

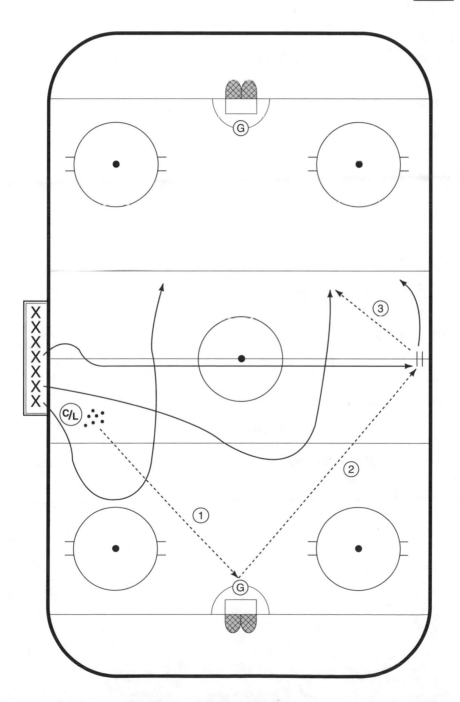

# 66 NEUTRAL ZONE OVERLOAD

## Purpose

- To practice controlling the puck in a confined space while avoiding obstacles such as other players

## Equipment   None

## Time   3-4 minutes

## Procedure

1. Split team in half, one group at each end.
2. On the whistle, three players come from each end (six total), enter and remain in the neutral zone, each controlling a puck while avoiding other players.
3. Encourage pivots, backward skating, and other variations.
4. On the next whistle, all six leave the neutral zone and go back to the end of the ice that they started from, while six new players perform the drill.

## Key Points

- Players must keep their heads up and be prepared to change direction, stop, or pivot while moving at high speed.

## Drill Progressions

- Have all six players inside the center circle only.
- Add chairs, pylons, or other obstacles.
- Have each player attempt a shot on goal when they come back into their end.

# NEUTRAL ZONE OVERLOAD 66

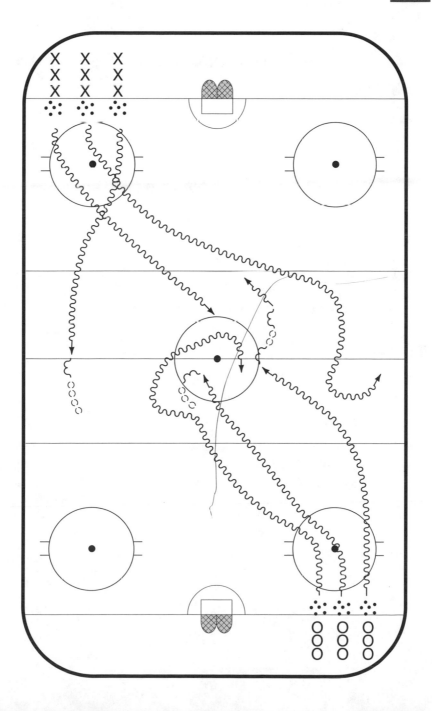

# 67 NEUTRAL ZONE BUMP

## Purpose

- To force players to gain control and pass as quickly as possible

## Equipment   None

## Time   2-3 minutes

## Procedure

1. Position four groups of forwards at the blue lines; each group has a puck. Position defensemen in two groups on side boards in neutral zone creating a half-ice drill.
2. Both ends begin on the whistle.
3. Defensemen (A) skate forward to midpoint of blue lines, stop, then skate backward toward center face-off dot.
4. Forward (B) passes puck to defenseman (A) who is skating backward. A quickly releases to player (C) skating across the blue line. C finishes with a shot on goal (numbers 1-3).
5. Forwards switch lines.

## Key Points

- Do drill at high speed, simulating a transition play in a game.
- Remind players to keep their feet moving.

## Drill Progressions

- Have defensemen join the attack and receive a second puck in corner (numbers 4 and 5).

# NEUTRAL ZONE BUMP

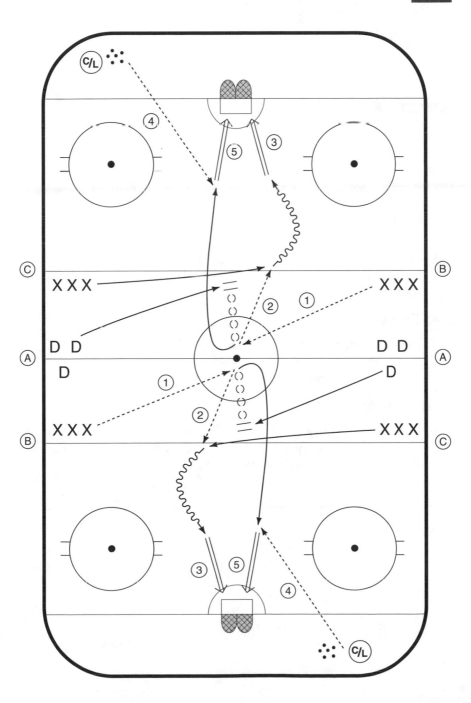

# 68 TRANSITION CHALLENGE

## Purpose

- To teach players when to turn from defense to offense as the puck is turned over

## Equipment   None

## Time   3-4 minutes

## Procedure

1. Five players per side begin in the neutral zone, with forwards skating randomly.
2. Defensemen skate forward to red line, then backward to their blue line.
3. Leader gives puck to one of the defensemen, who attempts to make the best decisions for moving the puck up ice.
4. Forwards must react and move to an open space.

## Key Points

- Defensemen should not force a pass. The best option may be to carry the puck rather than pass it.
- Forwards must read and react.

## Drill Progressions

- Before the drill begins, discuss with the defensive forwards ways to apply a specific system in the neutral zone, such as a staggered attack, to shut down the opposing team.

# TRANSITION CHALLENGE  68

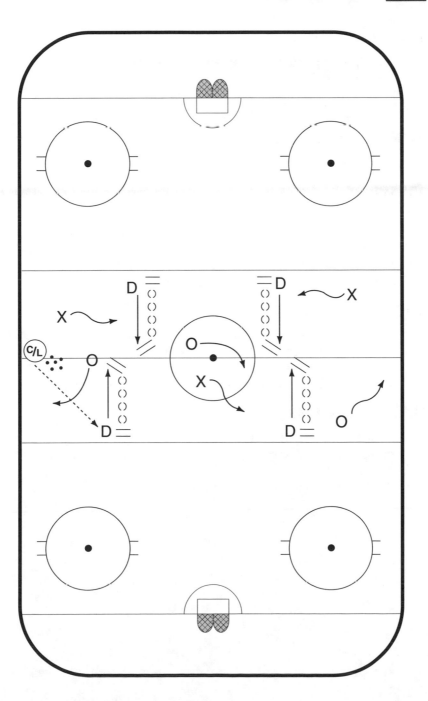

# 69 RUSSIAN THREE-NET

## Purpose

- To improve puck control in a unique situation with multiple options at high speed

## Equipment   Three nets

## Time   4-5 minutes

- 30 seconds per group

## Procedure

1. Place three nets on ice as shown.
2. Players come off the bench 5-on-5, with three pucks in play at the same time.
3. Players can score on any net during their shift.
4. Leader keeps track of goals for each team.

## Key Points

- If there are only two goalies, have an outskater play net, allowing them to challenge the shooters as well.
- Emphasize ice vision, encouraging players to switch direction at any time and go to any one of the three nets on the ice.

## Drill Progressions

- Designate a "shadow" for each group who will attempt to defend one player only, keeping that particular player from scoring any goals.
- Add a player on each side for a 6-on-6 game.

# RUSSIAN THREE-NET 69

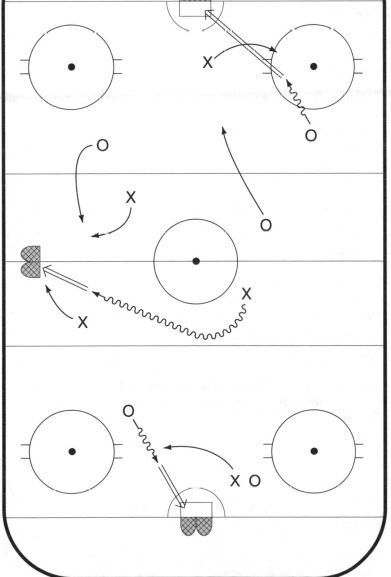

# 70 COACH'S CORNER

## Purpose

- To provide a variety of unique full-ice scrimmage situations
- To have fun

## Equipment   None

## Time   4-5 minutes (about 1 minute per shift)

## Procedure

1. Team is divided into two equal groups, with both groups seated at their respective benches.
2. Each team has a leader who calls any number from one to five, designating the number of players from his team on the ice for that shift.
3. Run a total of five shifts, using a different number of players each shift—never repeating the same number.
4. One leader blows a whistle to start a shift; at the same time, both leaders yell out the number they have chosen.

## Key Points

- A variety of scrimmage situations can develop, from 5-on-5 to 5-on-1, depending on what number each leader calls out.
- No one knows the number of players to jump over the boards until the leader announces it to his team.

## Drill Progressions

- Allow players to decide on combinations for themselves.
- Pull a goalie during a shift to add to a team's advantage.

# COACH'S CORNER 70

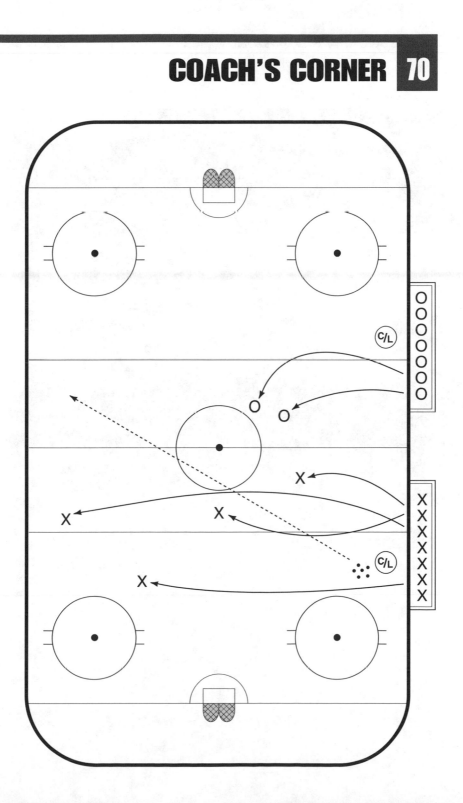

# 9 Sample Practice Sessions

To give you an idea of how to structure a practice using the activities in this book, I've provided some sample practice plans. When designing an effective practice session, coaches and players should first consider the following important factors.

- **Take time to prepare.** Have a general "game plan" for each practice session and share the objectives for that specific practice with players. Most players want to improve and please their coaches; however, it is difficult to do either if players do not understand what is expected of them. Always take the time to prepare and share your ideas with the players before you hit the ice.
- **Use the entire ice surface efficiently.** Rather than running all full-ice drills, split the ice in half, thirds, or even quarters, depending on the theme for that particular day. Ice time costs can be prohibitive in many locations, so it is important to make every second count toward skill development.
- **Break the team into workable groups**. Much like proper ice time use, players should be active for as much of the time as possible while on the ice. For example, a full-ice drill where only 2 players are active while 18 others stand motionless is not inclusive and rarely worthwhile. Break the team into smaller groups so that players can repeat each drill more often in the same amount of time.
- **Consider station work to reinforce specific skills**. Station-based learning is a popular concept in classrooms across North America, so why not try it on the ice as well? If the theme is individual puck control, divide the team into groups, each at its own specific drill station. Many of the drills in this book can be adapted to work in stations.

Before getting into sample practice sessions, let's look at how a station-based approach works on the ice.

# Three-Station Drill Session

The following example demonstrates how you might use stations as an effective means of practicing puck control for players of all ages—in this case, using a three-station drill. Station work is fun for players, yet it reinforces the basics of puck control. Variations of this kind of activity are endless and players will quickly understand the organization and sequence they must follow. As a progression, you might consider making the following activity a partner drill, where two players come out at the same time and try to maintain puck control between the pair.

In the following example, I have provided descriptions of the individual stations and flow of the drilling pattern as well. You'll find that by simply changing drill parameters, many of the activities in this book can work as station drills. Be creative and try station work as an effective way of drilling a hockey team.

## Guidelines for Three-Station Drills

- Split ice into thirds lengthwise, placing pylons to indicate the boundaries for each station (see diagram). Then split the team into thirds, each group going to one station.
- An extra net can be brought on the ice if you plan to finish the drill with shooting. (You do not, however, have to shoot in order to complete a drill.)
- Players go through the station and return to the same starting point, *making sure not to cross into another lane* (this can be dangerous if a high-speed collision occurs).
- Players return to the line by staying tight to the pylon boundary markers, making certain not to interfere with the next person doing the drill.
- Ensure that players understand how each station is run. Demonstrate the activity if possible.
- On the whistle, players rotate as a group to the next station.
- Total time per station is approximately 5 minutes, meaning the entire activity will take 15-17 minutes total.

### Deke Drill

Have a leader (C) standing on each blue line, forcing the oncoming player to maneuver, or "deke," while maintaining control of the puck. The person at the blue line may only skate laterally, not forward or

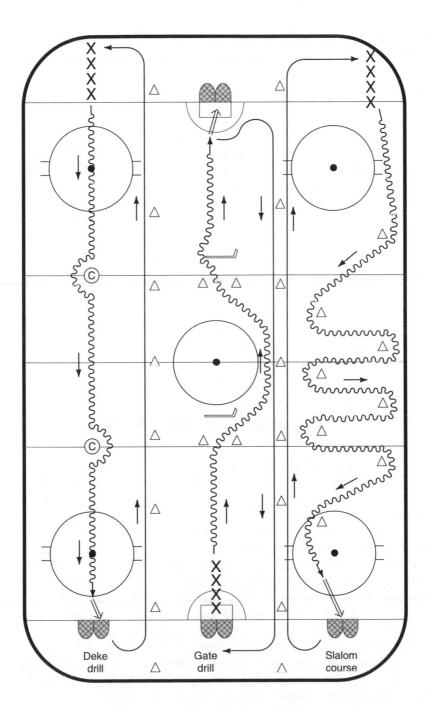

Deke
drill

Gate
drill

Slalom
course

backward. Depending on age and skill level, restrict the amount of contact—perhaps allowing only stick checking for younger participants.

### Gate Drill

Put two pylons approximately five feet apart at one blue line, with a hockey stick lying on the ice approximately three to five feet directly behind them. Set up a similar "gate" at the other blue line. Players must skate through the pylons and cut sharply in either direction while maintaining control of the puck. If you have help on the ice, have someone stand behind the gate and point in either direction as the player approaches. The player must react quickly and go in the direction as indicated by the leader. Make the drill more demanding by moving the stick closer to the gate, making the players cut in a more extreme fashion. Again, this depends on the skill level of the players involved.

### Slalom

Set pylons far apart, then have a series of three or four close together, forcing players to make quick turns, much like a slalom skier. Once a player is at the red line, the next person in line may begin.

# Sample Practice Plans

The following practice plans combine drills described in earlier chapters. These three examples demonstrate how you can approach one common theme, namely puck control, in a variety of ways and with differing specific objectives.

When putting together practice plans, remember that often a drill from one topic area in the book can easily be used or substituted for another part of practice. For example, a three-on-three activity could be used as a warm-up drill if done at a slower speed with no contact allowed. Experiment with different combinations, then seek feedback from players and fellow coaches about how effective a particular practice was on any given day. Never stop learning and trying new ideas. The perfect practice might be just around the corner!

For the following practices, add an extra 5 minutes for transition time between drills, and remember that most rinks have 10 minutes each hour allotted for resurfacing the ice.

# SAMPLE PRACTICE PLAN 1

**Total Time:** 60 minutes*
**Theme:** Puck control
**Objective:** To refine general puck control skills

| Drill Sequence | Time Required (min) |
|---|---|
| 1. **DRILL 18 — Canadian Skill Warm-Up** <br> *This is an effective, overall warm-up* | 5 |
| 2. **DRILL 3 — Skating the Egg** <br> *Skate with a partner* | 3 |
| 3. **DRILL 7 — Face the Flag** <br> *Get the legs moving in this full-ice activity* | 4 |
| 4. **DRILL 23 — Pivot and Go With Partner** <br> *Add shots at the end to warm up goalies* | 5 |
| 5. **DRILL 24 — Center Pivots** <br> *Again, finish drill with shots for goaltenders* | 3 |
| 6. **DRILL 54 — Webbie Cycle** <br> *Finish each cycle with a shot on net* | 5 |
| 7. **DRILL 55 — 3-on-3 Low** <br> *Players work on offense under pressure; you can discuss defensive concepts as well* | 10 |
| 8. **DRILL 47 — 3-on-3 End Zone** <br> *Finish the practice on a high note with a fun activity* | 5 |
| 9. **Recap, optional skate at the end, or free time** | 5 |

| | |
|---|---|
| Total Activity Time | 45 |

*Note: Includes 5 minutes transition time and 10 minutes to resurface.

# SAMPLE PRACTICE PLAN 2

**Total Time:**  60 minutes*

**Theme:**  Puck control

**Objective:**  To reinforce puck control skills in a fun environment

| Drill Sequence | Time Required (min) |
|---|---|
| 1.  **DRILL 9 — The Snake**<br>*Warm up; players should work on edge control during this activity* | 5 |
| 2.  **DRILL 12 — Pivot Warm-Up**<br>*Players should handle the puck skating both forward and backward* | 4 |
| 3.  **DRILL 22 — Turn and Go**<br>*Finish with shots to warm up goalies* | 4 |
| 4.  **DRILL 42 — Monkey in the Middle**<br>*Keeping score is optional* | 3 |
| 5.  **DRILL 49 — 3-on-3 Center Zone**<br>*Change players often, every 20-30 seconds* | 7 |
| 6.  **DRILL 57 — Power Play Challenge**<br>*Keep a running score after each attack* | 7 |
| 7.  **DRILL 69 — Russian Three-Net**<br>*Emphasis on quick transitions and scoring* | 10 |
| 8.  **Showdown (1-on-1 with goalie from center ice)**<br>*This is a great way to finish any practice* | 5 |

Total Activity Time    45

*Note: Includes 5 minutes transition time and 10 minutes to resurface.

# SAMPLE PRACTICE PLAN 3

**Total Time:** 60 minutes*

**Theme:** Puck control

**Objective:** To develop pressure puck control skills and enhance player conditioning

| Drill Sequence | Time Required (min) |
|---|---|
| 1. **DRILLS 25, 26, and 27 — Six-Line Drills**<br>*Warm up with a super progression to begin practice* | 7 |
| 2. **DRILL 31 — Face the Music**<br>*Players must always face same direction; require pivots* | 3 |
| 3. **DRILL 32 — Off the Hip**<br>*Players practice puck control in a 1-on-1 setting* | 3 |
| 4. **DRILL 33 — Wallpaper**<br>*This combines puck control and intensity to condition players* | 3 |
| 5. **DRILL 37 — Down the Wall**<br>*This game-like situation requires second-effort work* | 3 |
| 6. **DRILL 51 — 2-on-1 Attack**<br>*Player with puck must make good decisions while under attack* | 5 |
| 7. **DRILL 63 — Hoyer 2-on-2**<br>*This high-speed drill will test any age group* | 8 |
| 8. **DRILL 50 — Tire Shinny**<br>*Force players to maintain puck control AND positioning* | 10 |
| 9. **Cool down and stretch at center ice**<br>*Recap key teaching points during this time together* | 3 |

| Total Activity Time | 45 |
|---|---|

*Note: Include 5 minutes transition time and 10 minutes to resurface.

# Drill Finder

The Drill Finder acts as a reference for quick identification of the different aspects of puck control incorporated into each drill. Although the drills in this book have been organized within specific chapters that each deal with a unique aspect of puck control, in many cases you can use a drill to practice other skill areas or to provide more challenge. Remember to look at the "Drill Progressions" section for each drill for ways to adapt them to your own objectives. By focusing on the peripheral skills included in each drill, you may find it easier to organize efficient practices using a variety of themes.

| Drill # | Drill | Conditioning | Passing | Pressure | Contact | Pivots & Turns | Footwork | Speed | Fundamentals | Game Skills | Fun Activity |
|---|---|---|---|---|---|---|---|---|---|---|---|
| 1 | Stand Pat | | | | | | | | X | | |
| 2 | The Egg | | | | | | | | X | | |
| 3 | Skating the Egg | | | | | X | X | | X | | |
| 4 | Follow the Leader | | | | | | X | X | X | | X |
| 5 | The Imitator | | | | | | X | X | X | | X |
| 6 | Circle Drills | | | | | | X | X | X | | |
| 7 | Face the Flag | | | | | X | X | X | X | | |
| 8 | Dome Drill | | | | | X | X | X | X | | |
| 9 | The Snake | | | | | | X | X | X | | |
| 10 | Puck Control Pivots | | | | | X | X | X | X | | |
| 11 | Stretch n' Go | | | | | | | | X | | X |
| 12 | Pivot Warm-Up | | | | | | X | X | | X | |
| 13 | Alley-Oop! | | | | | | X | X | X | X | |
| 14 | Skate the Lines | | | | | | X | X | X | | |
| 15 | Dot Turns | | | | | X | X | X | X | X | |
| 16 | Quick Feet and Hands | | | | | X | X | | X | | |
| 17 | Four Blues | X | | | | | X | X | | | |
| 18 | Cdn Skill Warm-Up | X | | | | | X | | X | X | X |
| 19 | Noah's Warm-Up | X | | | | | X | X | | | |
| 20 | Obstacle Course | X | | | | | X | X | X | X | X |
| 21 | Snake Shadow | X | X | | | | X | | X | | |
| 22 | Turn and Go | | X | | | X | X | X | | X | |
| 23 | Pivot and Go | | X | | | X | X | | | | |
| 24 | Center Pivots | | X | | | X | X | X | | X | |
| 25 | Partner Weave | | X | | | | X | X | | X | |
| 26 | Forward/Backward | | X | | | X | X | X | | | |
| 27 | 3-Player Weave | | X | | | | X | X | | | |
| 28 | Puck Control Overload | X | X | X | | X | X | X | | X | X |
| 29 | Wall Pass | | X | | | X | X | | X | | |
| 30 | Pass Confusion | X | X | X | | X | X | | | | X |
| 31 | Face the Music | X | | X | | X | X | X | X | X | |
| 32 | Off the Hip | X | | X | | | X | | | X | |
| 33 | Wallpaper | X | | X | X | | X | | X | X | |
| 34 | Rabid Dog | X | | X | X | | X | | | X | |
| 35 | Stuff the Net | X | | X | | | X | | X | | |

| Drill # | Drill | Conditioning | Passing | Pressure | Contact | Pivots & Turns | Footwork | Speed | Fundamentals | Game Skills | Fun Activity |
|---|---|---|---|---|---|---|---|---|---|---|---|
| 36 | Blue Line Down | X | | X | X | | X | X | | X | |
| 37 | Down the Wall | X | | X | X | | | | X | X | |
| 38 | Circle 1-on-1 | X | | X | X | X | X | X | X | X | |
| 39 | Full-Ice 1-on-1 | X | X | X | X | | | | X | | X |
| 40 | Loop 1-on-1 | X | X | X | X | | | X | X | | X |
| 41 | Torpedoes | | | | | | X | X | | | X |
| 42 | Monkey in the Middle | | X | X | | | | | X | | X |
| 43 | Circle Relay | X | | | | | X | X | X | | X |
| 44 | Conditioning Relay | X | | | | X | | X | | | |
| 45 | Line Relay | X | | | | | | X | X | | |
| 46 | Sadler Double Barrel | | X | | | | X | X | X | | X |
| 47 | 3-on-3 End Zone | X | X | X | | | | | X | | X |
| 48 | 3-on-3 Goal Line | X | X | | | | | | X | X | X |
| 49 | 3-on-3 Center Zone | X | X | X | X | | | | X | X | X |
| 50 | Tire Shinny | | X | X | | | | X | X | X | X |
| 51 | 2-on-1 Attack | | X | X | X | | | | X | | X |
| 52 | 2-on-2 Low | X | X | X | X | X | X | | | X | |
| 53 | 3-on-3 All Back | | X | X | X | | | | X | | X |
| 54 | Webbie Cycle | | X | | | | X | X | | X | |
| 55 | 3-on-3 Low | X | X | X | X | | | | X | | |
| 56 | 5-on-2 Full Ice | | X | | | | | X | X | X | |
| 57 | Power Play Challenge | | X | | | | | X | X | X | X |
| 58 | Knob 5-on-5 | X | X | X | X | | | | X | X | X |
| 59 | 5-on-5 Breakout | | X | X | X | | | X | X | X | |
| 60 | 5-on-5 Situation Drill | X | X | X | X | | | X | X | X | X |
| 61 | Full Throttle | X | | | | X | X | X | | | |
| 62 | Speed Demon 1-on-1 | X | | X | X | | X | X | | X | |
| 63 | Hoyer 2-on-2 | X | X | X | X | | | X | X | X | |
| 64 | Four-Line Rushes | X | X | | | | | X | X | X | |
| 65 | Killer's Goalie Bump | X | X | | | X | X | X | | X | |
| 66 | Neutral Zone Overload | X | X | X | | X | X | X | X | | X |
| 67 | Neutral Zone Bump | | X | | | X | X | X | X | X | |
| 68 | Transition Challenge | | X | X | | X | X | X | | X | |
| 69 | Russian Three-Net | X | X | X | X | X | X | X | X | X | X |
| 70 | Coach's Corner | X | X | X | X | | | X | X | X | X |

# About the Huron Hockey School

Hockey has improved dramatically over the past 25 years, and Huron Hockey School, founded in 1970, has matched the sport's progression stride for stride as the leader in hockey instruction, both on the ice and in the classroom.

The Huron curriculum—annually updated, expanded, and now including a roller hockey component—is used internationally from San Jose, California, to Saint John, New Brunswick, with 30 campuses in between, and includes resident schools in Traverse City, Michigan; Potsdam, New York; and Cornwall, Ontario.

The seeds of Huron's dynamic growth can be traced to the hockey revolution that began in 1970, when Bobby Orr became the first defenseman in National Hockey League history to win the league scoring championship. While Orr's Boston Bruins went on to win the Stanley Cup Trophy that year, three young coaches realized the need for a more scientific approach to teaching the fundamentals of the sport they loved.

From the analytical minds of Ron Mason, now the all-time most winning coach in collegiate hockey; Bill Mahoney, former head coach of the Minnesota North Stars; and Brian Gilmour, an all-American at Boston University in 1967, evolved a now time-tested philosophy of hockey instruction by "professional educators": people who know how to *teach* the game and who know the little nuances that make a hockey instructor most effective. This concept of teaching hockey fundamentals has benefited more than 100,000 players, including over 350 who have made it to the National Hockey League.

Hockey has truly become a global sport, and Huron has become a global hockey school—one that prides itself on making kids better players. International exchanges have taken Huron staff members to Russia, where in 1965 Mason studied under the legendary coach Anatoli Tarasov, the father of Soviet hockey. Today, the school regularly welcomes youngsters from Japan, Italy, Sweden, Finland, Holland, Denmark, Germany, Austria, and France, who all come to learn hockey "the Huron way."

Paul O'Dacre
Director, Huron Hockey Group

# About the Author

K. Vern Stenlund is one of the world's leading hockey instructors. He has played professional hockey and coached the sport at all levels. Founder and director of the Hockey Academy in Windsor, Ontario, he is also a consultant to the Huron Hockey School, which he assisted in establishing satellite clinics in St. Louis; Bayonne, NJ; Chicago; Sun Valley, ID; Ridgefield, CT; and Jackson, WY. Stenlund has also conducted on-site coaching workshops at Ridgefield; Montreal; Sun Valley; and Cornwall, Ontario.

A first-round choice of the London Knights of the Ontario Hockey League, Stenlund led the team in scoring with 119 points during the 1975-76 season. The National Hockey League's California Golden Seals selected Stenlund in the second round of the 1976 NHL entry draft. He eventually played for the Cleveland Barons of the NHL and the Phoenix Roadrunners and Salt Lake City Eagles of the Central Hockey League. He also played for one year as a member of Bergen's team in the Norwegian Olympic Division League.

Stenlund began his coaching career directing the London Southwest Midgets of the Ontario Minor Hockey Association to a provincial championship in 1981-82. He was assistant coach at the University of Western Ontario in 1984-85 prior to coaching the Chatham Maroons of the Western Jr. "B" League for two seasons. He assisted in coaching the University of Windsor to the Final Four of the Ontario University Athletic Association in 1987-88. During the 1990-91 campaign, Stenlund directed the Windsor Bulldogs of the Western Jr. "B" League to a regular season title. Since 1992 he has been head coach of the Leamington Flyers of the Western Jr. "B" League, which has twice named him Coach of the Year.

Stenlund is an assistant professor of education at the University of Windsor. He received an EdD from the University of Michigan in 1994. A former area scout for the NHL's Mighty Ducks of Anaheim, Stenlund is a consultant for the Praxis Group (Provo, Utah).